383

They Carried the Mail

A Survey of Postal History and Hobbies

For Randy
—The best Bro. in the
Bay Area!
Danny

Christmas 1987

Mathew J. Bowyer

They Carried the Mail

A Survey of Postal History and Hobbies

Robert B. Luce, Inc.

Washington — New York

Dedication

In our patriarchal society it is somewhat a custom for a proud author to dedicate his book to his wife and children. I sincerely appreciate the time and inspiration my wife Virginia and our children Kevin and Karen gave me. But the family deems it only proper that this book be dedicated to all who shared in the endeavor.

Any perceptive person asked to name two people in the United States with the most complete knowledge of postal history and hobbies in their heads and at their fingertips, would surely come up with the names of Rita Lloyd Moroney and Carl H. Scheele. Mrs. Moroney is the Director of Research for the U.S. Postal Service and Mr. Scheele is the curator of philately and postal history for the Smithsonian Institution. Mrs. Moroney, an author in her own right, has worked closely, as a writer, researcher and editor, with the last five postmasters general—Messrs. Day, Gronouski, O'Brien, Watson and Blount. Throughout the world, the name of Scheele is synonymous with American postal archives and philatelic activities. His book *A Short History of the Mail Service* was published by the Smithsonian Institution Press in 1970.

This lady and gentleman, in addition to having a world of knowledge also cherish a great postal heritage in their hearts. For their help, I am indebted. I also wish to thank Miss Linda Wilson, researcher at Postal Service

Headquarters, for her help in checking facts and figures.

My book would be considerably less were it not for the dedicated people who consider their possession of extraordinary information and talents a trust which should be disseminated to the public.

Preface

We oldtimers who have considered mail a sacred trust do not want to hand the reins of our postal steeds to those who are inept and lackadaisical. Postal servants (an old-fashioned phrase which still carries the proper connotation) used to enjoy a status just a notch below the doctor, lawyer and minister. Abe Lincoln was proud to be postmaster of the little town of New Salem, Illinois. Being a postal worker was bonafide evidence of sterling character. But I am frank to admit that today public pride in the post office is not high.

I have tried to analyze the socio-political aspects that have brought about this change and to give the reader an insight into the vast, complex working of the U.S. government's largest civilian agency—its history, status and outlook for the future.

All civil service workers should have an interest in the conditions and future of this special group. The organized postal employees have traditionally been the driving wedge for beneficent legislation for all federal workers. Others look to this trail-blazing agency for signs of the times and a possible prognosis for their own particular group.

In my writing I have had to coin a new word: postology. There was none extant to encompass the wide spectrum of the subject matter oriented to mail, with which I concerned myself.

Since of necessity there is criticism and condemnation in the following pages, let me first go on record as believing, in spite of the complaints, our postal organization the best in the world. One trip to some place like Rio de Janeiro, where you stand in one line to buy stamps and in another to get at the glue pot, makes you appreciate our own system.

Contents

Part Four: Postal Practices

Part Five: Postal Corporation

Part Six: Postscripts

Appendices

Introduction

The postal service has touched the daily life of virtually every American for a period of well over two centuries. Any book on the subject is, therefore, always timely and of interest to a great number of people. Like other institutions with a long life span and with roots nourished in the soil of centuries, the postal service has had a colorful history. Grand traditions have been built and guarded; numerous legends have been fabricated and perpetuated. Post office stories have made their rounds with the mails, passed along from clerks to carriers. And it is most worthwhile that all of the pieces in the post-office mosaic be told once more and preserved on the printed page.

In this volume Mathew J. Bowyer has selected many of the brilliant episodes and curious facts from the rich storehouse of postal memorabilia he has accumulated during his long association with the service. Most importantly, the material is offered from the author's vantage point as an "insider." For that reason this work takes on added meaning at a critical time in the history of the U.S. mails, a period when the old Post Office Department is becoming the U.S. Postal Service. It is a time of transition from Federal agency to semi-official (or semi-private) corporation.

Moreover, the author is not the usual kind of "insider" who has written about the postal service in this century. He is not another J. Edward Day, Arthur Summerfield, or Daniel Roper—all former high-ranking postal officials who have authored works on the subject. Rather, Mr. Bowyer is an employee of the service who has spent a lifetime in the ranks of the system. Although Mr. Bowyer is an official in one of the nation's most important postal facilities, he remains close to the daily grind of the mail business. At the same time, his supervisory position and administrative vantage point at Dulles International Airport puts him uniquely in touch with the formulation of policy at high organizational levels. While he is situated close enough to Washington to remain keenly sensitive to the pulse of postal headquarters, his position has also enabled him to view the general activities from a comfortable distance and to retain a good measure of detachment or partisanship, as the case may be.

The view of the insider, after all, is vital to all who would study an institution as important as the postal service. In recent years the subject of communications has received increasing attention from scholars, writers, and the reading public. Happily, the study of postal communications has taken on more importance in America, finally breaking out beyond the limits of philately and the activities of studying postal markings and collecting picture postcards. Recent probings have become more comprehensive, more penetrating, more human. And while academic studies serve the reader very well indeed, the writings of participants in the ventures and adventures they describe are undoubtedly among the more interesting today and most valuable tomorrow.

Carl H. Scheele

Curator, Division of Postal History
Smithsonian Institution

1.   Tobacco Started the Mail Moving

On June 30, 1971, the U.S. Post Office Department, as such, died. Many had long looked upon her as a patient on her deathbed and were not sorry to see her depart this existence. As one of her faithful servants, though recognizing an incurable disease, I mourned her death knell. To determine the cause of death, to help other sufferers of such ills and comfort those she has left behind, I propose a post mortem beginning with a detailed history of the deceased.

An official American postal service was born in 1657 when the colonial court of Virginia required every planter to convey official dispatches to the next plantation under penalty of supplying one hogshed of tobacco for each default. This was the first action in the colonies to move mail from one locality to another and place responsibility for its transmission, as well as a penalty for failure.

It should be noted that this service pertained only to official dispatches. It would be another four years before the Virginia assembly required planters to forward "all letters superscribed for the service of His majesty or publique," or pay a fine of 350 pounds of tobacco. This action made postal service available to everyone in the colony—not just the government. It offered the same services to individuals in Virginia that the post office had provided for nearly a decade in the mother country.

Prior to this, the colonists handled their messages as best they could. Generally, ship captains hung leather satchels on the walls of the local taverns for the public to deposit overseas mail in, along with a monetary remuneration. All too often a tipler would use this open pouch as a means of replenishing his drink funds, thus contributing to the haphazard efficiency of the system.

A milestone had been reached on September 5, 1639, when the general court of Massachusetts, in an effort to provide a regular depository of mail from and to Europe, so designated the Boston tavern of Richard Fairbanks. He was to receive one penny for each letter handled. According to some historians, this made him the country's first postmaster. It was certainly the first postal system legally sanctioned by the colonists.

Postal developments were slow to reach America, despite the fact that letter delivery systems were operating in England and on the continent. The first serious attempt to establish a scheduled postal service between some of the northern colonies was in 1672 when the governor of New York, Francis Lovelace, directed a man to carry letters monthly between New York and Boston. The messenger was to travel by horse, and among other duties, he was "to detect and cause the arrest" of any runaway servants he might encounter.

Eleven years later the provincial assembly of Pennsylvania required officials to dispatch public letters within three hours of receipt, or pay a fine of twenty shillings for each hour of delay. In the same year, 1683, Governor William Penn established a weekly post between Philadelphia and New Castle, Del. Before the year was out, a continous post route was opened all the way from what is now Maine to Georgia.

By 1692, the population of the Colonies had grown to 200,000 and the first national postal system for the American colonies was authorized. According to British law, whatever services had previously been provided by the colonists themselves had been set up with assumed authority. On February 17 of that year, the Crown sold the American postal concession to Thomas Neale for a twenty-one year period, for six shillings and eight pence per annum. For good measure, Mr. Neale was also granted the postal concession for the West Indies. A favorite of the court of William and Mary and master of the mint, he never came to the colonies; an example of absentee proprietorship all too common in those days. Neale appointed Andrew Hamilton, a former Edinburgh merchant later to become governor of New Jersey, as his deputy to look after the Colonial postal interests, and in 1698 sold him his unprofitable concession. It then cost the same to mail a letter from New England to the West Indies or to Europe as to Maryland or Virginia. Mail took a week to make the trip from Boston to Philadelphia.

When Andrew Hamilton died, his son John was appointed to hold the postal concession. On John's death the Crown regained ownership. Thus from 1707 until the Revolution the General Post Office in London directly controlled—or more accurately, tried to control—postal operations of the American colonies.

Mail delivery somehow plodded along by the foot of man and beast until 1753, when Benjamin Franklin, postmaster of Philadelphia since 1737, was appointed by the English as a deputy postmaster general (jointly with William Hunter) for all the American colonies. Immediately service between New York and Philadelphia was increased to three times a week in summer and once a week in winter—a wonderful step forward. Two years later Franklin ordered mail dispatched between the colonies and England on a monthly schedule; and he saw to it that this was effected.

In 1758 Franklin ordered newspapers admitted as mail, and at standard rates. Prior to this they were carried without authorization by postmen who often charged exorbitant fees; moreover, postmasters who were also in the publishing business had their papers carried free. Those not so fortunate could only hope that the postman would accept their papers and they could afford the erratic cost. Franklin's act attested to his belief in the equality of all men and the virtues of competition.

Although Ben Franklin had performed his postal duties most efficiently, he was removed from his job in 1774 because of his questionable allegiance to the Crown. Revenue from the post by this time exceeded $15,000 annually; and the rather shaky foundation of our present postal system had been considerably strengthened.

As the American Revolution brewed, the job of postrider became steadily more hazardous. Not only were riders robbed but citizens who patronized the royal posts were threatened by rebellious colonists. A private mail system known as Goddard's Post—rivaling the Crown's service in thirty communities from Boston to Williamsburg—practically drove the British out of the postal business.

With ties to England broken, the Continental Congress resolved to have a postal system of its own and in 1775 appointed Franklin as its head with a salary of one thousand dollars per year. After the adoption of the Constitution, a postal service was duly authorized by the U.S. Congress. The act of September 22, 1789 created an official post and established seventy-five offices and the office of postmaster general within the Treasury Department. George Washington, four days later, appointed Samuel Osgood of Massachusetts the first postmaster general. However, for some time the postal system remained essentially what it had been under the British. It was quite common to find unofficial clerks at work, operating exclusively on a fee basis.

The Post Office was authorized as a permanent institution by Congress on February 20, 1792. Prior to this, the government had been undecided as to whether it should provide postal service, should leave it to each individual state, or put it out to be operated privately. In 1794 Congress authorized postmasters to hire letter carriers and pay them a two-cent fee for each letter delivered to a business firm.

But our fledgling postal service was by no means the first in the world. There is evidence that as early as 4000 B.C. the civilization in the Indus Valley had an organized message delivery service. Each succeeding civilization further refined the service. Remains of hieroglyphic writings on papyrus and fabrics have been found in Egypt which date to 3000 B.C. Their texts indicate they were messages sent from one place to another. Inscriptions on pyramids of about 1500 B.C. describe a letter delivery service that existed throughout the kingdom at that time.

Postal service is referred to in the Bible in 2 Chronicles and the books of Job, Jeremiah, 1 Samuel and 1 Kings. King Hezekiah had a postal service throughout Israel and Judeah and in the Book of Esther mentions the impressions of a king's signet ring on letters. Couriers, the postal service of that day, carried the epistles of Paul, Peter, Timothy and James.

In ancient times great importance was put on the use of seals. The oldest known is a clay seal used on letters delivered in Babylon in 3800 B.C. Today it rests in the Louvre in Paris. Seals served many purposes historically. The differing designs were easily recognized, even by the illiterate, and provided an emblem of authenticity. Also they were a deterrent to anyone other than the assignee having access to the contents. Today, when we use the term "break the seal," we hark back to a time when correspondence was sealed by a wafer of wax or other suitable material. Royalty and nobility had their own particular seal or coat of arms. Quite often this was engraved on a dauber made for the express purpose of affixing a seal on a letter or document. Or it was emblazoned on a ring which was used to "sign" an official article, which is how signet rings got their name. Today, it is still not uncommon, particularly in Europe and the Orient, to seal letters with personal emblems. And many families, even in the United States, cherish their little box with its sealing equipment as a treasured heirloom.

The ancient Greeks hired fleet-footed long distance runners to speed messages of their courier system. One of their champions, a messenger named Philonides covered sixty miles in nine hours. An official post served the Roman emperors. Letters in both these civilizations were written on sheets of wax or metal. The wax letters were easily altered but those on plaques of metal were considered authoritative. Thus the latin *sine cere* "without wax" came to mean genuine. It is the origin of the English word *sincere* and its use as a closing for letters.

The ancient Persians also had an official post. Cyrus, king in 559 B.C., developed a "top secret" way of dispatching confidential information. A courier's head was shaved and the letter stained onto the scalp. He was locked up until his hair grew out and then sent to his destination.

Nearly five hundred years before the birth of Christ, the Greek historian Herodotus described the postal system of the Persian king Darius the Great: "Neither snow nor rain nor heat nor gloom of night stays these couriers from the swift completion of their appointed rounds." This statement of the pomp and splendor of a noble service can be read today on the facade of the general post office in New York City.

Succeeding emperors throughout the known world had their official posts. But at the end of the third century A.D., when Diocletian opened his service to the public, it was the first so available in Europe.

In 1100 Kublai Khan established an efficient postal

system in China which lasted for six hundred years. It
was an extension of the system of the days of Confucius,
improved by Genghis Khan—Kublai's grandfather. Under Kublai Khan the system encompassed ten thousand
post officies, all in communication with each other, principally by horseback and occasionally by boat. It was
available to anyone who could read and write. On the
other side of the world, by the fifteenth century the
Aztecs were operating a mail service in Mexico.

By the end of the Middle Ages means for the distribution of private mail was available in most of Europe.
Notable among these was a mail system which the house
of Thurn und Taxis began operating about 1400 in Austria. In 1460, Roger of Thurn und Taxis was granted
rights to operate a post between the Tyrol and the Italian
states. The same family opened a private post between
Vienna and the Netherlands in 1505, and in 1516 they
were given the imperial Austrian concession to operate
between Vienna and Brussels. Their couriers were given
permission to carry letters for individuals in 1544, and
by 1560 this service developed into a legalized and regulated monopoly. Eventually their postal system served
most of Europe, with the Counts of Thurn und Taxis
deriving part of their profits from acting as postmasters
general for the countries they served. The family made a
lucrative living for four and a half centuries, until the
various European posts were taken over by their governments. Today the descendants of this family have
highly valuable philatelic items, but their name has come
to be more widely associated with a brand of Bavarian
beer.

Lawmakers have traditionally pre-empted rights to
private postal services whenever they became profitable.
In 1644 Edmund Prideaux was given authority to operate a mail service in England at his own expense, with
the understanding that he might keep any profits. Within

six years, the British government was charging £ 10,000 per year for this right; and by 1660, asked £ 21,500 from the lessee.

Postmaster General Bishop of England, in 1861, invented a date-stamp device with which to postmark mail. This oval stamp imprint was designed to speed delivery of mail, on the theory that a letter bearing its mailing date stamped by a post office would be noticed if delayed. The stamp was first used in London, Dublin and Edinburgh before moving to British colonies in India and North America.

In 1680 a British merchant, William Dockwra established a penny post in London. He carried letters and packages up to a pound in weight and ten pounds in value, registered and insured, for only a penny. He opened a chain of several hundred receiving stations, collected the mail each hour of the day, channeled it into seven officies where it was date stamped, sorted and sent out for delivery, making six deliveries a day in the suburbs and as many as ten in the business district.

Although losing money while developing his business, he soon began showing a profit. Thereupon the Crown, asserting its sovereign monopoly, forced him to pay damages to the Duke of York, to whom the postal revenues for that area were due. Then Dockwra's services were incorporated into the official post office.

Until the twentieth century, any letter was considered an important paper worthy of exacting and proprietary handling in keeping with the standards of the times. The day that the mail was due was called the Post Day and was an occasion—almost a holiday—for the townsfolk to assemble to receive mail and have the newspapers read aloud. In some countries the mail was heralded with the blowing of trumpets. The present insignia of Sweden's postal administration—a fancifully fluted horn— honors the tradition of postilions announcing arrival of the mail. Even today in wooded hollows in the mountains in rural America, there are a few families who rely on the postmaster to read their mail to them and render his learned opinion on its contents. Possibly it shall always be thus.

2.   Postal Reform: Stamps and Envelopes

The first half of the nineteenth century saw a great expansion of the U.S. post—its services and its employees. Three notable events happened in 1825. The term Post Office Department acquired official sanction. The service had been called the General Post Office—identical with the British postal service then and now. More notable was Congressional authorization for the delivery of mail to private homes. However, the carriers were to be paid by the people to whom the letters were taken, not by the government. If a patron didn't desire this service, he could notify the postmaster and thereafter pick up his mail at the post office. This system was to last for about forty years. Finally, the establishment of the Dead Letter Office indicated how comprehensive postal service had become.

The prestige of the department climbed in 1827 when the salary of the postmaster general was raised to that of the heads of government departments. Within two years the postmaster general was made a member of the president's cabinet and was no longer under the Treasury Department. Even more status followed. The Post Office had now become large enough and important enough to be a real political plum.

The mails were highly political. Precipitated by previous incidents in which postmen withheld mail from opposing political factions, in 1836 congress found it necessary to pass an act forbidding mail to be withheld from anyone.

Prior to 1837, each postmaster general could choose a seal of his particular liking. Most of them favored a depiction of the wing-footed god Mercury, in Roman mythology the messenger of the gods as well as god of commerce and travel. Generally the figure would hold a serpent-entwined staff or caduceus. In 1837, the Post Office Department adopted an official seal which depicted a mounted horse at full gallop. The public has erroneously assumed this to be symbolic of the days of the Pony Express which did not come into being for another twenty-three years.

At this time things were happening in England which would affect American mail service. In 1837, Rowland Hill—inventor, publisher, scientist, educator—published a pamphlet titled "Post Office Reform: Its Importance and Practicability". This discussion of postal matters advocated prepayment of postage and the postage stamp, which he called a label "with a glutinous wash on the back."

His pamphlet also recommended that letters go anywhere in England for only one penny. He held that lower costs would increase sales, thereby affording more economical operations. Postage rates then varied with the distance and weight. Four pence had been charged for a single sheet of paper weighing no more than an ounce, going not more than thirty miles. Rates graduated upwards to a maximum of one shilling eight pence each piece of paper traveling over four-hundred miles.

At this time, the paper of the letter itself was simply folded and the folds secured at the interstices by the application of a sealing wax. Naturally letters, papers or documents that were intended to be more prestigious were more artfully and expensively prepared. Thus the use of ribbon in the seal, as our diplomas so formally exhibit, was evolved.

The adoption of Rowland Hill's proposal in 1839 caused many changes in the British postal service. Paper bags were authorized for patrons to enclose their letters; and the bags would be marked to show that the postage had been paid. Around 1650 another Englishman named Hill—John Hill, an attorney at York—had set up a private post for packages and letters, and proposed that letters be carried to any place in England for one penny. It is ironic that it took nearly two centuries and another person of the same surname, who as far as is known had no knowledge of his namesake's plan, to effect this idea.

In September of 1839, the British Treasury sponsored a public contest for suggestions on how best to handle the prepayment of postage. They received nearly 3000 entries and awarded four £ 100 prizes, considering the money well spent and helpful to the problems.

Hill's postage stamps and wrappers were first put to use in 1840. That first stamp showed a picture of Queen Victoria and was dubbed the "penny black." More important than the physical act of prepayment of postage were the implications of this new idea. It was now possible to have confidential communications by mail. No longer did the sender have to come under the scrutiny of the receiving postal employees. He could mail a letter without officialdom knowing the mailer. This was a new-found freedom which proclaimed the sovereignty of each citizen. Eventually, because of this pamphlet Hill was given the Order of the Bath, a national award of twenty thousand pounds and many other accolades. In death he was given the ultimate honor: burial in Westminster Abbey. Today, his idea of adhesive postage stamps is hailed as one of mankind's greatest inventions.

At this time, local mail was still very often handled by private citizens as an informal business. But in 1841, in the city of Philadelphia, an agency known as Blood's Dispatch was organized to handle local mail. It had the distinction of issuing the first private postage stamp in

the United States. In January of the next year, Alexander
Greig started a similar firm in New York City known as
the City Dispatch Post. He sold his own three-cent stamps
for local delivery. His private post took so much business
from the official New York post office that the government bought out his business after less than a year's operation. The only change the government made was to
precede the firm's name with *United States*.

Beginning in 1845 the cities of Alexandria, Baltimore, New Haven, New York and St. Louis issued
stamps—known as postmaster's provisionals'—at the
discretion of the postmaster. This up-and-coming practice of local stamps without federal warranty was contrary to U.S. law, which required that postage be paid in
cash during post office hours. Nevertheless, stamps were
a convenience and the postmaster general's office turned
its head.

Russia had the distinction of introducing stamped
envelopes, or lettersheets, in 1845. Originally only for the
use of the nobility, they soon were allowed for all. The
United States was not to adopt stamped envelopes until
seven years later. In 1847, Wheeling, Virginia (now
West Virginia) precancelled some stamps—another philatelic first.

Encouraged by England's success with stamps and
the continously enlarged demand for private postage
labels in this country, the United States government, on
July 1, 1847, put out its first issue of a postage stamp
duly authorized by Congress. A five-cent adhesive showing Benjamin Franklin and a ten-cent one showing
George Washington were the first stamps prepared for
nation-wide use. In that year about 7 million letters were
handled—an average of 6 for each citizen. This may be
contrasted to 1971 with an average of 415 pieces of mail
for each man, woman and child in the United States. In
1849 the first American patent for envelopes (No. 6055)
was issued to Jesse Parker and Cornelius Watson.

With the discovery of gold in California, there was an immediate mass stampede to the area. The resultant population explosion in the West caused the first mail to be transported overland across the United States. It arrived in Los Angeles in May of 1848. To profit from the gold rush—so it was charged—the price for a letter to the Pacific Coast was increased from ten to forty cents. Having been bitterly criticized for the exorbitant charges, in March of 1851 a flat rate of three cents prepaid or five cents COD for a letter weighing not more than half an ounce and not going more than three thousand miles was announced. The charge was double for greater distances or overseas. It is interesting that Congress authorized the minting of three-cent coins on the same date that the change was made to three-cent postage.

On April 1, 1855 prepayment of domestic postage became compulsory in the United States; it had been optional since 1847. Probably contributing to its eventual requirement was the anecdote that when Zachary Taylor was nominated for president by the Whigs, his sponsors thought he had rejected the invitation. They received no response from him. It was later determined that the notification had been sent COD, and Mr. Taylor made it a practice to accept only prepaid mail!

Effective January 1, 1856 prepayment had to be with postage stamps. Also in this year, the fee for letters over three thousand miles was raised to ten cents and registered mail was inaugurated in the United States to provide more security for valuables. An improved stamp perforating machine was patented by the Bemrose brothers and soon put into use by a Philadelphia stamp printer. Unknown at the time, variations in perforations were to become an area of study within philatelic circles.

Two years later the first U.S. patent for a postmarking and stamp cancelling machine was granted. By 1858 the street letter boxes, which had been in use for three years in London, were being set up in the United States. Things were happening fast. On July 1, 1859 the balloon *Atlantic* became the first aircraft to transport mail in the United States. Professor John Wise carried a sack of privately posted letters from St. Louis headed for New York City, but was forced down in a windstorm near Henderson, N.Y. before reaching his destination. The mail was thrown overboard but washed onto the beach at Oswego two days later, and was given surface dispatch and delivered undamaged.

At the end of the decade, the tempo of the times was such that there could be no doubt as to the never ending future of the Post Office. The infant nation hadn't even had its first centennial but it was already seen that, with the grace of God, nothing could stop its growth.

3. $5 in Gold per Letter

The 1860's inaugurated perhaps the most glamorous era in the history of American mails. The famous Pony Express, a private postal and express system, started on April 3, 1860. It ran from St. Joseph, Mo. to San Francisco, Calif., via Sacramento. Horses were changed at 190 stations within the 2000-mile route which normally took eight to ten days to cover. The Pony Express was the fastest means of communication available during its day; and this permitted them to charge as much as five dollars in gold for the delivery of a half-ounce letter. Contrary to general assumption, the enterprise lost money—free enterprise money, not the taxpaper's.

Great importance was placed on letters, and it was understood that a carrier would risk his life to get the mail through. Many of these valiant postriders were shot from their saddles as they galloped through hostile Indian country. There are tales to stir the imagination, of riderless horses arriving at the destination with the all-important letters still in the saddle bag.

For all its fame, the Pony Express lasted less than two years. In October of 1861, the telegraph lines from the East met with those from the West. This marked the end of the Pony Express which had been providing an ever-decreasing circuit of fast communication routes in areas where the telegraph lines had not yet been erected.

Stamps were rapidly becoming common and the hobby was so widespread by 1860 that dealers began sending out lists of stamps for sale. The first such list is credited to Oscar Berger-Levrault of Strasburg, France. In this year, also, the Scott Stamp and Coin Company, publishers of the *Standard Postage Stamp Catalogue* used throughout America today, started business.

In 1861 Lincoln entered the presidency. His postmaster general, Montgomery Blair, was probably responsible for more important changes in the U.S. mails than any other man who has held the position. He introduced four major innovations: free city delivery, postal money orders, railway post offices and Rural Free Delivery.

During the Civil War all minor coins disappeared from circulation and the Treasury issued stamps to be used for coins. A man named John Gault patented a small brass case with a transparent front to hold a stamp used as a medium of exchange. He was very successful making these for private businesses which wished to have their advertising shown on the reverse.

In July 1862, the first railway post office began to operate in the United States, although railway mail service was not officially inaugurated until 1864. The first such mail had been dispatched in 1830, in England.

About the same time, Joseph Briggs, the assistant postmaster and window clerk of Cleveland, Ohio, in an unsanctioned personal service on his part, gave letters to storekeepers to deliver to their customers and personally delivered mail to residents in his city. The Civil War made mail, particularly from soldiers, especially important. Brigg's enterprise was so gratefully received that he wrote the postmaster general informing him of the public's reaction. The postmaster general then invited Briggs to Washington where they both presented this new concept of service to Congress. And, in March of 1863, at the urging of Lincoln and Blair, Congress authorized free city delivery to go into effect on the first day of July. Mail was to be delivered to private homes with the carriers being paid by the government.

In 1864, Mr. S. Allen Taylor began the *Stamp Collector's Record,* the first American stamp newspaper, which was published for ten years.

That same year, a money order system was authorized by Congress immediately upon its proposal. It was instituted so money could be sent to soldiers and they could send part of their pay back home. The service was extended to foreign countries on an experimental basis in 1867, and officially in 1869.

By 1868 we had 26,481 post offices, a figure which would increase each year until 1902. The cost of running the U.S. Post Office was $22.7 million per annum, reflecting the increased tempo of operations. Though a tremendous amount at that time, this would cover only one day's expense in 1971.

At Promontory, Utah, on May 10, 1869, the railroads met. They had started, as had the telegraph lines, from both east and west. As the telegraph caused the end of the Pony Express, the rail hook-up marked the end of stagecoach mail along these routes.

In the 1870's, the U.S. Post Office expanded its volume but without startling innovations. It became an executive department of our federal government on June 8, 1872. The postal card was introduced in the United States in 1873 after having been born in Austria in 1869 and coming into use in Germany in the following year. A federal law prohibiting sending obscene literature in postal matter was also passed in 1873 and free delivery of mail was finally given to all cities with a population of at least twenty thousand.

In 1874 the Universal Postal Union was founded at Bern, Switzerland. The purpose of this organization is symbolized by a statue in that city. The sculpture shows figures representing the continents clasping hands around a globe. This signifies the nations of the world offering their mail facilities to the people of other nations. Universal Postal Union agreements provide that a letter may be mailed in one country, with that country's postage, and be delivered on a reciprocal basis by another country. Prior to this, every country handling foreign mail wanted their own postage on the article also. Just one year after the U.P.U. was founded, international parcel post was introduced. This was thirty-eight years before parcel post within the borders of the United States was to be authorized.

Exemplifying the continual quest to improve mail service was an 1875 experiment in Nevada using imported camels to carry mail across the desert.

In the 1880's more postal services were added, and increased use of railroad post offices sped the mail on its way. The first serious attempt to remove patronage from government jobs was made in 1883 when the Pendleton Act created the Civil Service Commission. Also in 1883 the United States reduced postage rates to two cents for each half-ounce letter carried to any part of the United States or its territories.

A number of innovations were started in the United States in 1885: Special Delivery, stamped newspaper wrappers and envelopes bearing a request for return if not delivered. Postage rates were again reduced, this time to two cents per ounce for letters and one cent per pound for newspapers.

The earliest date for which postal records are available in the United States is 1886. At that time the volume was less than 5 percent of today's and the revenue was only 0.3 percent of what it is today. But postal operations were greatly enlarged the next year when towns of ten thousand people became eligible for free delivery.

In the late nineteenth century the railway mail car became the backbone of the American postal system. It was the heyday of the road clerks—those in the Railway Mail Service (eventually becoming the Postal

Transportation Service). These employees were one pay grade higher than ordinary postal clerks and worked in railway mail cars, terminals, transfer offices and other facilities where extensive mailroute memorization was required of the clerks.

From the 1880's until the mid-twentieth century, practically every place in the nation received its mail from the railroads—if not directly, then from an off-loading point. The very small places often had no post office and therefore were not shown in official post office guides. Nevertheless, the clerks were expected to put this mail off at a place where it could be delivered.

The postal transportation clerk had to know which train took the mail for each individual town in his distribution area. The expertise of mail routing was on his shoulders. Among the tools of his trade was a little book, one for each state or geographical area, published by Rand-McNally and purchased by all conscientious clerks who worked mail for that area. The publishing firm would obtain listings from the railroad companies, of every town, village, hamlet and crossroads through which their lines passed. Then this information would be correlated into a list showing every possible way of getting a shipment to any town.

The Post Office Department, by regulation, upon the discontinuance of an office would drop its name from their books after three years. But the "Rand" would continue to list it with an explanatory note and even showed the former names of places when the name changed. This little booklet, which fitted into the hip pocket, was an invaluable aid to the postal technician who cared. It provided the information necessary for him to identify the "nixies," supposedly undeliverable items.

The service of the road clerks was considered the acme of postal perfection, and in their knowledge of distribution and their finesse in handling the mails it was. The clerks considered all letters special—as if imagining in the upper left hand corner the schoolboy inscription, "If not delivered in five days, try like hell the sixth." As the smoke-belching passenger train roared through a town where it didn't stop, an iron hook mounted on a swivel was thrust out the doorway of the mail car to seize a mailbag hung up on a specially constructed pole over the station platform. The suspended pouch was jerked into the moving train while townspeople watched and waved at their link with the rest of the world. As he snagged the "catcher pouch," the clerk in the RPO kicked another pouch off the train. It contained mail for the local office that the clerks had worked en-route. My choosing to become a postman was probably influenced by the nostalgic call of the train whistle in my own hometown.

When road clerks were in their prime, being a postal employee had some hazards it doesn't have today. In 1887 mail trains were in 248 accidents. Altogether, 108 mail clerks were injured and 4 killed. In 1889, 193 railway mail clerks (3.5% of the total) were either killed or seriously injured in rail accidents.

In true pioneer spirit, the road clerks consoled themselves that things were worse in other countries. In 1889, the postmaster general of Bengal province, India, complained that he couldn't quite keep things going; man-eating tigers had consumed eight of his carriers during the past year. And in Morocco the hundred and fifty miles across mountains, desert sands and bridgeless rivers between Tangier and Fez were crossed on foot in three and a half days. The carriers were issued short lengths of rope which were to be tied to a big toe and ignited when stopping to rest and sleep. This assured that they would be awakened in three hours.

In 1889 the first Post Office on wheels made its maiden run in Carroll County, Maryland. It was designed to bring all postal services, e.g. sale of stamps and money orders, to the farmer's home. In 1894 the Bureau of Engraving and Printing of the Treasury Department took over the job of printing postage stamps from private firms.

In 1896 Rural Free Delivery was authorized, beginning with five routes in West Virginia. This was brought about in large part by the political power of the Grange associations, which argued that the farmer was being discriminated against since city dwellers had free delivery and were more able to get their mail from the post offices than were the rural dwellers. Practically everyone conceded that this expanded service would boost the economy of the country, but they dreaded the cost. Since the economy of the country was basically agrarian, the farmers wielded the balance of power and got their way.

As our country came to the close of the nineteenth century, it offered undreamed-of opportunities. The mail service, already serving to unite the nation, was now in a position to do its part in making the United States of America the greatest republic in the world.

4. More Post Offices and Better Service?

The twentieth century opened with the U.S. Post Office Department bursting with health—a strong, growing, up-to-date organization ready, willing and able to serve the public well. In 1901 the department counted 76,945 offices, the largest number to this time.

Although the uniformed postman at the turn of the century enjoyed great dignity, he often suffered for the sake of sartorial splendor. Not until 1901 did the Post Office relax its dress regulations which required that in addition to coats, vests were to be worn regardless how torrid the weather.

In 1902 Rural Free Delivery became permanent and its carriers came under Civil Service. Prior to this they had been appointed by their congressmen subject only to the approval of the people they served. Appointees were now required to take a written test; but the examining officer, the rural agent (forerunner of the postal inspector), was allowed to give consideration to intangible factors such as personality, in arriving at the final score. By 1909 there were more than forty thousand rural routes in the United States.

Back in these early days of our emerging transportation network, mail contracts were often let without specifying the mode or means by which the mail would be transported. The department designated this type of contract in their bookkeeping system with an asterisk. This

is how the term *star route*, which stands today, came
about.

Indicative of the times was the *way pouch*. In many
areas the mail hauler would bring this *working* bag of
mail in turn to each postmaster on his route, who would
take out the letters he could deliver in his bailiwick, and
add the outgoing mail that his office had generated.

In 1910 a postal savings system was authorized to go
into effect the following year. It was designed for immi-
grants from Europe accustomed to saving at post offices
in their home country. Postal savings encouraged thrift,
and paid two percent interest annually. Persons only ten
years old could open an account with one dollar, or begin
a savings card with ten cents. The cards were promoted
in elementary schools throughout the nation.

In 1913 insured mail service became established and
parcel post was instituted. Mail carriers had been permitted to carry parcels in addition to the mails, and they
did this profitably as a sideline. The official service was
a means for the government to collect that revenue it had
been missing from parcels. The United States had been
behind major foreign countries in parcel deliveries. Prior
to 1913, at port cities in the United States, packages
could be mailed to foreign countries—only to destinations
within the United States was the service not officially
available.

Postal service, then as always, was molded by the
needs, capabilities and limitations of the times. Early
history shows humans acting as runners to speed a message by foot, then the use of horses and, as demand and
availability arose, of dog sleds, boats, trains and trucks.
In the early twentieth century, mankind had progressed
to airplanes.

The field of aviation was just opening in August of
1911 when French aviator Jules Vedrinnes made news
flying letters from Paris to Deauville. In the United
States the first authorized airmail flight took place the

same year. On September 23, Earle L. Ovington flew from Garden City to Mineola, N.Y.

But 1918 was the real beginning of airmail. On March 20 the first regular service in the world was established between Vienna and Kiev with intermediate stops at Cracow, Lemberg and Proskurow. Regular airmail service got off to a poor start in the United States. On May 15 as President Woodrow Wilson watched expectantly, the plane failed to start for the inaugural flight between Washington, D.C. and New York City. Someone had forgotten to gas it up. This remedied, the Army pilot got into his open cockpit, flew for twenty-five miles and then broke his propeller in an emergency landing. The next day he tried to complete the flight but got lost, ran out of fuel and landed near the Chesapeake Bay. Refueling, he tried again but crashed near his destination and the mail had to be trucked in.

This "snafu" had one final, unexpected aspect. Some of the stamps issued the day before that first flight depicted the plane flying upside down—a bonafide error for which a few lucky people later thanked the Post Office.

After this inauspicious beginning, the Army operated one round trip every day except Sunday on this route. On May 15, 1968 the Post Office Department issued a commemorative stamp marking the fiftieth anniversary of this first scheduled flight; at least it began that day.

The Air Commerce Act of 1926, designed to promote civil flying, gave an impetus to aviation which promoted airmail service. The following year private aviation companies were given contracts to fly the mail in the United States and airmail service was established from San Francisco to Manila via the *China Clipper*. But the first transatlantic airmail flight was not until May 20, 1939—the twelfth anniversary of the Lindbergh solo across the ocean.

Denoting the glamorous era of early airmail, in 1930

a U.S. Airmail flag was adopted for display on buildings at airports handling airmail. The gold-fringed flag showed, superimposed upon a white background with a blue lower and upper border, a pair of golden wings flying a golden globe between a set of bold red stripes. Just prior to World War II, this beautiful flag was one of only sixty-eight current emblems of the United States. It is significant to note that once aviation became commonplace, this emblem was forgotten—only twenty years after its inception.

In the interest of efficiency, on April 28, 1904, legislation was passed authorizing the postmaster general to allow the mailing of certain matter without postage stamps affixed. This permitted postage meters to come into use. There was a slow moving away from postage stamps until Pitney-Bowes introduced postmark ads or meter slogans in 1929. That changed things. By 1957, revenues from metered postage began to exceed revenues derived from the sale of stamps and postal stationery.

Beginning in 1932 when it went from two to three cents, the letter rate in the United States began a steady climb. In 1958 it went to four cents, and in 1963 to five cents. The 1968 postage rate of six cents seemed quite high until one considered it a restoration of the minimum rate in effect in 1792.

In a continual search for improved methods of transportation, the first highway post office was put into operation on February 10, 1941. It ran on a 184-mile route between Harrisonburg, Va. and Washington, D.C. The en-route working of the mails paralleled the operation of railway post offices and the mail could be delivered directly to the doors of offices far removed from railroad tracks.

This type of service reached its peak in the 1950's when nearly two hundred routes were in operation. A decline was brought about in the 1960's by a new concept of working mail at concentration points. Soon, practically all the highway post office routes including the original, were eliminated. The concept of railway post offices lasted nearly a hundred years, but the highway post office mode of mail survived less than thirty.

World War II brought major innovations. To speed the shipment of mails, a postal zoning system was placed in operation in 1943 in 124 of the larger cities. Then modern photographic technology was called upon to produce V-Mail, a process designed to conserve weight and space in overseas shipments. Letter sheets were photographed and the negatives miniaturized. A film strip containing nearly two thousand messages weighed only 5.5 ounces when ready for shipment; a similar number of ordinary letters would have weighed about 50 pounds. The negatives were turned into full-size prints before delivery at the destination.

At the end of the war, international air parcel post was started the same year as domestic air parcel post: 1948. More than sixty countries from the United States to Europe, South America and the U.S. territories and possessions were united in this one year.

In 1953 airlift service began. Mail not paid at the air rate was transported on a space available basis with the airlines charging the government a reduced rate which made this haulage as economical as surface transportation.

In 1955 the Certified Mail began. It provided a record of delivery and receipt without the necessity of registering or insuring the mail. Also in that year Combination Mail was started. This allowed a letter paid at the first-class rate be attached to a package paid at a lower rate.

Considering all these advances—and the efficiency with which an ever increasing volume of mail was handled, the public thought the postal service of the 1950's had reached a pinnacle of perfection. Perhaps they were right.

I have a friend who says he can reveal the exact date and hour when the U.S. Post Office Department began to decline: November 10, 1958, at 11 A.M. At that moment a uniformed postman delivered a small brown package insured for one million dollars to the Smithsonian Institution in Washington, D.C. Inside was the fabulous Hope diamond; a gift to the U.S. government from New York jeweler Harry Winston. Aside from fame for its value, the Hope diamond is equally noted for the bad luck it brings to all who have it in their possession.

5.   Upside-Down Plane Sells for $100,000

Since 1840 when England issued the first gummed postage stamp, the penny black, people have collected stamps. The wealthy have been able to let it become an obsession, and the common man has found in the pursuit a needed escape or a relaxing pastime. Though it does take financial wherewithal to pursue a hobby of collecting anything adequately nowadays, an interest in philately may be satiated with only the observance and study of stamps. It is truly a hobby that anyone can pursue.

Originally, stamps were so unusual that the sheets had instructions for their application printed on the margins. Now, with the increasing number of stamp-issuing countries and the great range of subject matter on their stamps, collectors are almost forced to specialize. At the turn of the century there were fewer than ten thousand different issues of stamps in the world. Today there are probably a million. Even if he had the money, no individual would have time to categorize specimens of every item issued.

Specializations center about individual interests. A botanist might collect stamps depicting plants issued by any country in the world; a Civil War buff, stamps of that era; an athlete, stamps showing sports. Philately has something for everybody.

Philately is the hobby of those who are fond of stamps. The word is coined from two Greek words—a combination of *philos* meaning fond, and *ateleia* meaning

41

an object free from (further) tax, or more clearly, prepaid fees. The derivations of postal terms are equally interesting.

Look at the origin of the word *stamp*. We are all
familiar with the press with which a notary public em-
bosses his seal on paper. In historical England, the same
thing was done to show the tax on official documents was
paid—except their tools required more pressure and had
to be stamped with the hand, as we now do a stapler. The
gummed bits of paper which were invented to replace the
stamping or embossing of a seal were first called *labels;*
but common usage appropriated the word stamp to replace the original name of the handy decals.

Next consider the word *mail*. It was given to us by
medieval society—the material of the bag used to carry
letters. It was a flexible fabric woven of interlocked metal
rings, generally worn by knights to ward off offensive
blows. Since letters were so valuable, they too were pro-
tected by mail.

During the opening years of this century while
postal collecting was still young, the hobby became almost
a craze. Newspapers ran daily columns on the subject and
radio stations featured philatelic panels. Renowned public speakers, billing themselves as philatelists, toured the
major cities and captivated their audiences with fascinating tales about stamps.

Did you know that postage stamps represent in
themselves a form of negotiable currency? Since they
were first invented, stamps have been used throughout
the world in lieu of money, particularly during periods of
low coinage. In the latter part of the nineteenth century
during the South African gold rush, stamps instead of
coins were the rule rather than the exception. Also at that
time, the South Pacific islands of Tonga and Hawaii used
stamps for money. In the twentieth century stamps came
to be used for coinage in Saudi Arabia, (1925); Russia
issued cardboard stamps (1915–1918) bearing the in-

scription that they were to be considered on a par with
silver coins; and stamps were used for currency in China
(1939).

Stamp collecting was spawned by the intelligentsia;
but once born, all of society kept it growing. Franklin
Delano Roosevelt and his postmaster general James Farley—both avid stamp collectors—used to stop the presses
and take out sheets of stamps before they were perforated, to autograph and present to friends. Such liber-
ties were stopped when philatelic associations pointed out
that the practice was improper and brought financial
windfalls to the recipients.

To the serious stamp collector, the hobby is a science
as well as an art. He will probably subscribe to a trade
journal and belong to an organization such as the American Philatelic Society, the largest national stamp group.
In examining stamps he may use a perforation guage.
By international agreement stamps are recorded in cata-
logues in several ways, one of which is the number of
small round holes between stamps for easy separating.
Universally, the standard measure is the number of
perforations in a distance of two centimeters. Thus if
somehow a few stamps of a certain issue were discovered
to have seven perforations in this distance when they
were supposed to have eight, the rare kind would be comparatively more valuable.

The collector will recognize a *roulette*, a separation
provided by straight slits cut in the paper between
stamps. A variation of this perforate called a *serrate
roulette* is placing the slits to form a sawtooth edge. Im-
perforate stamps are those that have no perforations at
all. Any unintended variation of perforations would be
quickly observed and the issue would command a premium price.

Even the adhesives used on stamps is a specialty.
There has been a plethora to excite the senses of taste,
sight and smell. Amongst less palatable concoctions have

been fish glue, dextrose, tapioca and synthetics. At one time Cuba flavored her stamps with strawberry and vanilla. There are suggestions continously both serious and joking, for a taste of everything from aphrodisiacs to beer and wine. In line with the times, in 1968 Great Britain started giving users of stamps a lick with a kick. Their printing firm replaced the traditional gum-arabic mucilage with an adhesive that contains a bit of alcohol.

Oddly shaped stamps attract many people. They are more fascinating when one realizes the shape served a purpose. The first triangular stamps appeared in 1851 in Africa and it is said they were so shaped to be readily identifiable by postal workers who couldn't read.

The collecting of American stamps becomes greater with each passing production, regardless of complaints about recent designs. From the starter collection of stamps purchased by the schoolboy to the U.S. government's treasures on view at the Smithsonian Institution's Hall of Philately and Postal History, society recognizes the import of this subject. Mail Americana provides an interesting means of learning and enjoying our country's history. Probably the most far reaching laws pertaining to U.S. postage stamps is the requirement that no living person may be portrayed on the stamps and that any unused stamp issued since 1861 is still good for its face postage if not mutilated or defaced.

According to the U.S. Postal Service, all stamps may be broken down into five categories. Regular stamps range in denomination from one-half cent to five dollars. Traditionally they depict former presidents, other prominent persons and national shrines. A regular stamp usually remains on sale about ten years. Memorial stamps are issued to honor American statesmen. Typical examples are John Kennedy and General Eisenhower. Airmail stamps are for airmail postage only. The history of aviation is usually shown on these. Special stamps are sold to prepay fees for special services other than regular or airmail postage. Commemorative stamps were first issued in 1861 (envelope stamps), with the mucilage version beginning in 1893, to honor events and persons associated with the development of the nation, including statehood anniversaries.

To further classify stamps there are such terms as mint, used, unused, coil, overprint, surcharged, precanceled, etc. Knowing how to properly describe the items is part of the game.

Thousands of ideas are submitted annually for new stamps. One man figured a good way to lick the crime problem would be to show the FBI's Wanted on stamps. Rejected! Another thought a first class stamp idea would be one honoring totem poles. Accepted! It is noteworthy that Lindbergh is the only living person ever honored on a U.S. commemorative stamp. A 1927 ten-cent airmail stamp showed Lindbergh's name but not his likeness.

With the ever increasing search for new ways to bring money into national treasuries, all countries now realize the value of the philatelic sales of stamps. There is a business eye on profits made by the stamp-sized principalities of San Marino, Liechtenstein and Monaco. For many years they have gleaned major revenues from stamp collectors.

As a sign of the times, Great Britain, that bulwark of conservatism who once arched an eyebrow at other countries' profiting from postal issues, has finally joined the parade. For years she has only showed the head of the monarch on her stamps and still does not spell out the name of the issuing country—a prerogative of the place where postage stamps started. New stamps designed to attract collectors, are now the order of the day. As an indication of the extent of the trade, Britain's post office now grosses about eleven million dollars per year through the sales of its first day covers, presentation packs, commemoratives and special issue stamps.

Commemorative revenue can be traced to 1888 when

New South Wales stumbled upon a new idea and produced a set of ten stamps honoring the centenary of the
founding of that colony. Hong Kong followed, commemorating its fifty years under British rule. Within ten
years, twenty-two countries had issued commemoratives.

This type of stamp became increasingly prolific and
reached some sort of a high in this country, in 1948, with
the issuance of the chicken stamp, honoring the centennial of the American poultry industry. The design featured a chicken with the three cent denomination
enclosed in an oval. This stamp caused a lot of ill will.
One reason was, contrary to the advertised sex of the
fowl, close scrutiny revealed it to be not an egg-laying
hen, but a rooster. This issue resulted in the curtailment
of indiscriminate commemoratives. Today the United
States issues between ten and fifteen annually from
about three thousand requests. Each new commemorative
nets about one-half million dollars from collectors.

In the United States, the philatelic sales section at
the main Washington, D.C. post office operates a mail
order and over-the-counter service with sales of about
three million dollars per year. In addition to this, millions
of stamps are sold to collectors by post offices throughout
the nation. They all cut the postal deficit, as it costs only
about a dollar a thousand to print the stamps.

Exotic means of mail transport kindle the imagination and whet the appetite for more information. At
various times in this country letters have been hauled by
camels, donkeys, dog sleds, dirigibles, balloons and
rockets. One that particularly strikes the fancy is pigeon
post, the transmission of letters by carrier pigeons. These
letters, called *flimsies*, are collectors' items today.

During the War of 1870, pigeons were used with
moderate success to get messages out of beseiged Paris.
Fifty-seven of 363 pigeons returned with messages. However, the physical characteristics of many areas in the
world have made this at times the best means of convey-

ance. In 1897 the postal authorities of the United States experimented with pigeon post in the Hawaiian Islands. In Ceylon, in 1964, a former prime minister Dr. W. Dahanayake suggested in parliament that if his country could not provide better telephone service, it should revert to the pigeon post they used a hundred years earlier. Carrier pigeons can cover a distance of 160 miles in three hours, a fact not designed to soothe the ruffled feathers of a patron complaining that it has taken three days to deliver his letter posted no further away.

Collectors value almost anything that bespeaks differences. The island of Tonga in the South Pacific is encompassed by coral reefs and no sea-going boat can come to the dock. There the ocean current, running north to south, is put to work as a mail carrier. Incoming mail is dropped into the water in tin cans north of the island and washed ashore; and out-going mail is pushed into the sea south of the island where the boat fishes it aboard. It is all marked Tin Can Mail. Many collectors wouldn't consider their collection complete without one of these covers.

As the space exploration program got into high gear, it was natural to think of shooting mail from one area to another. This has been done, though simply as an attention-getter which served no useful purpose. The mail was shot by rocket from the sea off the coast of Cape Canaveral (Kennedy) onto land and retrieved. And in 1969 it was seen fit for astronauts Armstrong and Aldrin to carry a handstamp a quarter million miles on their space flight to cancel man's first piece of mail on the moon with the slogan Moon Landing, U.S.A.

Commemorative issues are perennial collectors' favorites—but often they remind the public of unintended things. In May 1968, a stamp was issued bearing the caption Law and Order. A couple of months later PMG Lawrence O'Brien, under whose direction the stamp was issued, resigned to manage Hubert Humphrey's presidential campaign. Later in the year when the third party candidate George Wallace chose law and order as his slogan, he found it emblazoned on a commemorative stamp—issued by a postmaster general of the opposing political party!

Due to the great scientific advances made in printing processes, the chances of printing errors on stamps are remote. But since more than twenty-six billion postage stamps are printed each year in the United States, we should expect errors to pop up now and then and they do. In 1962 the background color on some of the Dag Hammarskjold commemorative stamps printed in this country was upside down. To flood out the rarities, the stamps were re-run incorrectly, which set a precedent for modern stamp making.

Aside from printing errors, there is the fallibility of design. The chicken stamp was not alone. In 1970 a schoolboy noticed that the commemorative showing the Pilgrims of 1620 included a flag which did not exist until 1801. The seventy-fifth anniversary of the first transcontinental railroad was honored on a postage stamp that showed the smoke from the locomotive blowing in one direction and the flag in the opposite. Any attempt at explanation tends to publicize such an issue, so officialdom wisely ignores discussion.

We are not the only country to make errors. In 1969 a Munich stamp dealer caused much embarrassment to West German postal officials when he pointed out that the new stamp issued to commemorate fifty years of airmail service in Germany, showed a three-engined Junker 52 with registration number D-2201: the plane used by Hitler in his 1932 election campaign.

Of greater political impact was a stamp issued in 1900 by the Dominican Republic showing a map of the island of Hispaniola, divided between the Republic of Haiti and the Dominican Republic. The artist had shown the boundary line extending into Haiti's territory. This resulted in fighting between the two countries which lasted for thirty-eight years; and it is estimated that fifteen thousand lives were lost because of that stamp.

Stamp collecting is big business, and dealers in philately know all the angles. An old regulation stated that postmasters of first class offices must send to Washington all foreign stamps taken from the dead letters that accumulated at their offices. Over the years U.S. stamps started arriving, too. They were auctioned off every six years. So during the last sale at the main post office in Washington, in September, 1967, seventeen hundred pounds of stamps were auctioned in lots containing about ten pounds each for an average price of nineteen dollars per bag. Altogether, the sale netted $3,270 from the couple of hundred dealers and private collectors— some had flown in from as far as the West Coast for the auction.

Around the turn of the century a popular method for church organizations to raise money was to solicit used stamps from business houses having a large correspondence. The organization would then sell the stamps by the pound to the dealers. These lots were known as "mission mixtures" and some rare stamps have turned up in this manner.

Some postal enthusiasts are fortunate enough to inherit valuable specimens. The Queen of England inherited a fabulous stamp collection from her grandfather, George V, who used to spend three afternoons a week keeping it in order. It consists of approximately a thousand album pages worth at least three million dollars. Stamps, like other collectors' items, are enhanced by age.

Many successful American businessmen found their business acumen extended into stamp collecting. The collection of Josiah K. Lilly, grandson of the founder of the Lilly pharmaceutical firm, was sold by his estate in 1968 through the New York auction house Robert A. Siegal

Co. for a record-breaking $3,134,127. One of the major
items was a 1925 regular ten centavo stamp called the
"black Honduras." Its sale price was $29,000 because it
was overprinted with black Aero Correo 25.

The year 1968 was a landmark for stamp sales. In
October, at a sale in London, half of a stamp was sold for
$408. Half of a penny one at that! The stamp, issued in
Grenada, West Indies, in 1883, had been cut diagonally
and used as postage on halfpenny mail, a practice valid
in the past in several countries. In November a pair of
Canadian twelve-penny stamps issued in 1851 to cover
the cost of postage from Canada to the British West Indies was sold at an auction in New York to a Toronto
dealer for $39,000. These two stamps, showing the like-
ness of Queen Victoria, were part of 147 lots sold for a
total of $236,000 at this sale by the Harmer Galleries.

In addition, an envelope bearing two Mauritius one-
penny stamps of 1847 was sold in New York for
$380,000, the highest price paid for any one item at a
philatelic auction. And on February 8, 1968, a corner
block of the prized 1918 twenty-four cent stamp showing
an upside-down Curtiss Jenny biplane was sold for
$100,000, the highest price ever paid for an American
philatelic item. One hundred of these stamps were sold
before the press error was detected. Today each com-
mands a price of $30,000.

In March 1970 a group of investors paid $280,000
for a one-cent British Guiana printed in 1856 and re-
puted to be the world's most valuable stamp. Since being
found in 1873 by a twelve-year-old schoolboy, this stamp,
the only known one of its kind, has brought successively
higher prices whenever it changed hands. The prior
owner had bought the stamp in 1940 for a mere $42,000.

Though we are all born with a need for a hobby
above monetary value, I imagine it is the secret ambition
for all stamp collectors to find a valuable specimen.
Searchers have scoured everywhere, even advertising in

out-of-the-way places to buy old filing cabinets of correspondence, with the unannounced aim of finding a rarity. Though probably most all of the exceptionally rare ones have been found by now, it isn't inconceivable for a few to turn up. The more your knowledge of the subject, the greater your chances of being that lucky one.

6.   "Missionaries," Saints and Christmas Stamps

What is the most desirable subject for stamps, according to the consumer public? Anything concerned with religion! The largest postal collecting association in the world is the St. Gabriel World Federation. It is an organization of collectors of mail items with a Christian theme; Protestants, Catholics and Jews all belong to the fellowship. The late Francis Cardinal Spellman, a renowned collector of religion on postage stamps, was an honorary president of this organization and the philatelic museum bearing his name at Regis College in Weston, Mass., features his personal collections. When the famed churchman was given half a million dollars to be used as he wished by Mabel Gilman Corey he had the museum erected to house religious philately.

About a thousand churches and cathedrals have been depicted on stamps, as have some hundred and fifty saints and famous Christians, as well as numerous symbols and emblems relative to Christianity. Many collectors specialize in Marian collections, devoted exclusively to the Virgin.

Unfortunately, people will capitalize on anything and religion is no exception. In 1956 the Republic of Panama began issuing a series of 261 stamps, showing all the popes since Saint Peter. The stamps had too high a value to be used for postage. Clearly, it was a scheme to make money from the vast number of collectors of religion on stamps.

52

The versatility of missionary ministers has created legends and rarities. In 1895 a British preacher, the Reverend E. Millar in Mengo, the capitol of the Uganda Protectorate in Africa, included running the post office in his duties. When the capitol was moved to Entebbe, the Rev. Millar was isolated. Undaunted, he began to produce his own stamps, the values being shown in cowrie shells, a strong currency in central Africa at that time. This man had two typewriters, an amazing fact in itself considering the place and time; so he typed his stamps. These rarities of the first order, although not pictorially representing religion, are part of religious philately.

Religion enters the making of stamps. Every detail of their manufacture must be designed to avoid offending their users. Some stamps are printed on paper with watermarks, which may be brought out by certain chemicals. A simple way is to float the stamp face down in a saucer of benzine or lighter fluid. In 1888 Sudanese Camel Postman stamps were watermarked with a lotus-blossom design. Zealous of their Mohammedanism many Sudanese saw the watermark as the subtle injection of a foreign religious symbol into their personal lives. The stamp had to be withdrawn immediately.

Around 1900 the Arabs took offense at an overprint in Hebraic characters on stamps issued by Palestine. They thought this implied British recognition of Palestine as the land of Israel. To pacify the Arabs, the British courts handed down a formal ruling that the stamps did not affect Arab rights in Palestine as far as the British were concerned.

In 1930 Czechoslovakia came out with a stamp honoring religious reformer John Huss. Bohemian Catholics became quite angry that a man who had been burned at the stake should be honored on a stamp. Czechoslovakia recalled the stamps.

Postal paper sold for a price above that for carrying the mail with the overage accruing to a designated cause

is known as semi-postal or charity postage. This category
is often included under the heading of religious philately
because the semi-postals are frequently sponsored for re-
ligion-oriented causes. A famous Belgian issue supported
the restoration of a ruined abbey. Though most foreign
governments have raised money for various causes in
this manner, the United States has refrained from so
doing.

When a philatelist talks of the high price of missionaries he will probably be referring to the second
most-valuable type of stamp in the world—Hawaiian
missionaries. The Hawaiian Islands was one of the first
countries to adopt postage stamps even though very few
were used, and those almost exclusively by the missionaries. Today a single specimen of one of these stamps
will sell for several thousand dollars.

The use of religious themes on postal stamps in the
United States touches on the matter of our American
principle of separation of church and state. In cases of
dispute the government is forced to stand on the First
Amendment to the Constitution, which states: "Congress
shall make no law respecting an establishment of religion, or prohibiting free exercise thereof . . ." As in so
many areas of jurisprudence, the terminology is considered ambiguous. So, there is a hue and cry from a
sizable portion of the citizenry whenever the federal government, through its post office, makes any reference to
religion through its stamps. Notwithstanding in 1948
the United States issued a commemorative stamp titled
Four Heroic Chaplains. These men—a Jew, a Catholic,
one of the Reformed Church and a Methodist—gave their
own lifebelts to the men without when the American
troop transport *Dorchester* was torpedoed and sunk by
the Nazis off the coast of Greenland in 1943.

In 1965 there was a U.S. commemorative for the
hundredth anniversary of the Salvation Army, and in
1963 there was a stamp commemorating the Red Cross—

by necessity carrying the symbol of Christianity. Incidentally, in Turkey the counterpart to our Red Cross anti-tuberculosis stamps, uses, instead of a cross, a red crescent—the symbol of Islam.

Although various nations of the world have been issuing special stamps for the Yuletide season for many years, the United States did not come out with a Christmas issue until 1962, when it produced a four-cent stamp showing a wreath and candles. Immediately the Christmas stamp program ran into trouble, mainly because not enough had been produced. But although the stamps were more symbolic than religious, certain non-Christians opposed the program from its inception.

In 1963 we had a painting of the nation's Christmas tree on the ellipse in Washington. This brought charges that Christmas was being used for the furtherance of politics. In 1964 we had the holly, mistletoe, poinsetta and pine cone stamps. The mistletoe was attacked as a pagan symbol; and many people complained it was a waste of money to issue four different designs. The 1965 Christmas issue depicted the angel Gabriel. Many complained the angel looked more like a Hollywood sexpot with too heavenly a body for an angel.

In 1966 the Christmas stamp controversy reached its peak with the printing of the Memling painting of the Madonna and Child which hangs in the National Gallery of Art. The main protests came from the American Jewish Congress which said that it violated the constitutional requirement of church-state separation. But a billion stamps were sold in 1966 and the department knew they had a winner. So they announced a double-sized rerun of the stamp for Christmas of 1967. Immediately a Washington court was asked to enjoin the Post Office Department from issuing it. Notwithstanding that the art work is appreciated universally, a suit was brought by the Americans United for Separation of Church and State on the ground that the stamp involved

the use of tax money toward "the establishment of a religion." The stamp was alleged to be a Roman Catholic
depiction because it featured a missal. U.S. District
Judge Holtzoff, a Jew, heard the case and ruled in favor
of Postmaster General O'Brien.

A record one and a half billion copies of the 1968
Christmas stamp were produced. They were run off on
the Bureau of Engraving and Printing's new three million dollar nine-color web press. It took half a million
pounds of paper for this stamp showing fifteenth-century
Flemish artist Jan Van Eyck's *The Annunciation*, the
angel Gabriel greeting the Virgin Mary as described in
the scripture of Saint Luke.

Possibly to avoid partisan criticism, the 1969
Christmas stamp was a simple winter scene of bygone
days by an unknown artist with the word *Christmas* on
the margin. But 1970 saw a return to a block of four different stamps. These featured antique toys. In addition,
a fifth stamp devoted to the Nativity was issued. Two
Christmas stamps were issued in 1971. One was a part-
ridge in a pear tree designed by Jamie Wyeth. The second
was a reproduction of Giorgione's *Adoration of the
Shepherds*.

Society's aims and aspirations have been and will be
chronicled in its postage stamps. Each bears an official
imprimatur and those of a religious nature particularly
tell the temper of the times. For man's actions—what he
shows and says—is what religion is all about.

7.   Collectomania from Hell to Jerkwater

As a general practitioner must have at least a speaking acquaintance with medical specialties, so a philatelist is familiar with the sidelines of his profession. He will be a postal historian as well as a hobbiest. He knows such things as the difference between post cards and postal cards; the first is privately printed and the second is sold in post offices. He will know that, technically, if non-postal stamps bear on them an indication of their value in money, they are to be called revenue stamps. If they bear no specific indication of money they are tax-paid stamps.

Revenue stamps, sometimes called fiscal stamps, are issued for a variety of purposes. Real estate and stock transfer stamps are examples. Though federal laws place them under the Treasury Department, they are viewed as being postally related. Documentary internal revenue stamps were sold at post offices until December 31, 1967. They are now purchased, exchanged or redeemed at district offices of Internal Revenue. Additionally, a number of states issue stamps to show the tax has been paid on certain of their levies.

Nationally, tax-paid stamps were first issued in 1862 and were required on many items to help pay the cost of the Civil War. Now they are found only on merchandise such as whiskey and playing cards. The cork or cap on an alcoholic beverage bottle is sealed with the tax stamp and packages of cards are closed in a like manner.

A good philatelist will have considerable knowledge of printing methods. This is the only way to classify some stamps properly. The most common method of printing is from an engraved plate. The desired design is cut into the surface of a metal plate. Ink is worked into those lines on the press; and when dampened paper is pressed onto the plate, the ink is transferred to the paper and tends to stand up from the surface, giving its characteristic appearance.

A letterpress uses an exactly opposite technique. The ink is applied to a raised surface. When observed from the back, the stamp will show a raised pattern where the type has pressed into the paper. Lithography is more complicated. The design is put on the plate by a photographic process which produces slightly greasy lines. When dilute acid is poured onto the plate it will not adhere to the greasy lines but covers the non-design part of the plate. The acid solution repels ink which sticks only to the lines. When paper is pressed against the inked plate only the lines of the design appears. A lithographed stamp feels flat and almost slick.

Each plate used by the Bureau of Engraving and Printing in printing stamps has a control number known as a plate-block number. This has produced another hobby: collecting stamps still attached to the ordinarily disposable edge of the sheet on which this number appears. The same plate-block number is shown on all four corners of the sheet so that when the sheet is cut into quarters, properly called panes, the number will appear on each quarter. Panes generally containing fifty or one hundred stamps, are the form in which stamps are delivered to post offices for sale. The usual method of collecting plate numbers is to buy a block of four stamps with the number attached. Some collectors want specimens of the same number in all four positions. A set of blocks with identical numbers in each position is known as matched plate blocks.

Until the advent of the Giori printing press, it was necessary to use a different plate for each color on a stamp. This necessitated as many plate numbers in each corner as there were colors. The Giori press, first used for the flag stamp issued on July 4, 1957, makes it possible to print any number of colors from the same plate. But in runs where there is a danger of colors overlapping, more than one plate, with different numbers of course, is still used. The Florida Quadricentennial issue of 1965 was such a stamp. Collectors of plate numbers pay particular attention to the different numbers and the quantities printed of each.

To kill the stamp and prevent its re-use, the Post Office authorizes various marking devices. The resultant figures on stamps and envelopes are the subject of many collections. Today the usual cancellation is a circle that encloses the place where mailed, the date, A.M. or P.M. and possibly the zip code. Attached to this circle are lines called killer bars, intended to line over the stamps. Any variance from the usual cancellation is a collectors' item. Some collectors save railway post office or highway post office cancellations. Some want those struck aboard ships at sea or those showing Army post office marks. Each special category has its fanciers.

In the formative years of our Postal Service, many original cancellations were devised by local offices, some of them made from hand-carved devices. They showed everything from a "kicking-mule" to Masonic emblems. These imprints and the tools to make them are desirable items and present unique displays of mail Americana.

Today the Postal Service rigidly controls all cancellations, but does, upon occasion, authorize slogans to be added to the canceler. Some are limited to certain communities for specified periods to publicize special events.

Postmarks are interesting for many reasons. A let-

ter postmarked Coos Bay, Oregon reminds one that this
was the westernmost spot in the United States—until
Alaska and the Hawaiian Islands were given statehood.
Everyone notices a letter bearing a postmark with an
interesting placename, especially if it is affixed with unusual stamps. An English stamp with the head of Shake-
speare would be enhanced if further examination showed
the letter was postmarked at the bard's birthplace:
Stratford-on-Avon.

The variety of placenames is one reason postmarks
have such appeal. In the list of U.S. post offices there are
a couple of Hells (W.Va. and Wyo.), but no heaven.
There are places named Trinity in four states—Ala-
bama, Kentucky, North Carolina and Texas. Four places
bear the designation devil: Devils Elbow, Devils Lake,
Devils Slide and Devils Tower. Did you know mail can be
postmarked Truth or Consequences, N. Mex.; Rough and
Ready, Calif.; Two Gun Town, Ariz.; Tombstone, Ariz.;
Bird in Hand, Pa. and Sleepy Eye, Mont.?

Placenames with a Yuletide flavor take on an added
significance when the special Christmas stamps go on
sale. According to custom a post office with a seasonal
name like Christmas, Fla., or Santa Claus, Ind. is selected to put these stamps on sale a day before they may
be sold in the rest of the country. These offices do a boom-
ing business in postal cancellations for collectors at that
time of the year.

Showing the name of the place where mail is deposited is a matter of ego for most communities; but any
attempt to discontinue the practice meets a powerful opposition. After all, every place has to have some distinction. Caribou, Maine, besides being a potato shipping
center, is the nation's northeasternmost city—distinct
from Anchorage, Alaska, the northwesternmost city, or
St. Augustine, Fla., the oldest city. Citizens in every community look with disfavor upon any scheme to infringe
upon its individual name and with equally strong dis-

favor of the encroachment of the ciphers upon society. They feel if the accounting office presses its anti-postmark campaign too far, then it can go to 54872. A society that denies individuality denies freedom itself.

One of the most sought after categories of postal collecting—and one often overlooked—is that of mail franks. These signatured wrappers are wanted by collectors of autographs, government mementos, mail and stamps. According to autograph dealers, franking signatures are a most salable bit of Americana and collectors are anxious to purchase new finds, even present-day items.

The origin of the frank goes back more than three hundred years. King James I of England granted free mailing privileges to members of Parliament and certain of the nobility. These people soon began to misuse their privilege and transported all manners of items—laundry, livestock and even household furniture—to the detriment of the Post Office's fiscal well being. Eventually, some even sold letter covers with their franking signature to others for profit. The situation became so bad that the postal reform of 1840 abolished the franking privilege for all except Queen Victoria and a few officials.

In America, as in Britain, the frank has been used and abused. Many times a franked signature was converted to an I.O.U. by swindlers. To prevent this many holders wrote *free* between their given name and surname. *B. Free Franklin* was not a case of Ben Franklin alluding to freedom from the English government as overly romantic historians would have you believe, but rather to prevent his franking signature from being misused.

In 1775, Congress granted the franking privilege to members of the Continental Congress and to military

personnel. In 1887 it was abolished because of cheating.
In 1891 it was given back to congressmen. In 1895 it was
extended to the vice president because he was the president of the Senate and should get the same consideration
as its members. Today the vice president of the United
States, vice-president-elect, members of the Senate,
sergeant-at-arms of the Senate, clerk of the House and
former vice presidents are authorized to use the frank
for six months after the expiration of their term of office.

The franking privilege is also extended to ex-presi-
dents and widows of presidents. But no president of the
United States since U.S. Grant has had the franking
privilege. Instead they may use an envelope imprinted
with the words "Official Mail, Penalty for private use
. . ." The president must use postage on his personal
mail.

The expert collector will know a lot about postal history. He will be able to tell you that because PMG John
Wanamaker felt the residential letter carriers wasted
too much time "waiting for the servants to answer the
doorbells," in 1890 the post office began experimenting
with mail boxes on the porches and slots in the front
doors. Before it was over with, every home in the nation
had a letter box! The old ones, of course, are collectors
items.

As a child I remember a record titled "Letter Edged
in Black," playing on the graphinola. The lyrics included
a passage that went something like this: "He rang the
bell and then he blew the whistle . . . and he says, Good
Morning to you, Jack, as he handed me that letter edged
in black!" Those words typify a bygone world. The postman doesn't ring your bell anymore, nor does he blow a
tweeter. Times change. Any important mail he delivers
to you may be lost amongst the circulars and advertisements. And many people no longer know the meaning of
the black-edged letter—now a collectors item.

Oddly-addressed envelopes have been made into exhibits by collectors of mail Americana. In the post office of yesteryear solving puzzle addresses was a game. Sometimes a play is made on geographical oddities such as the states of Colorado and Wyoming being the only two having unbroken straight lines as their four boundaries. A letter directed to Tar Heel went to North Carolina. Buckeye went to Ohio and Hoosier to Indiana. People in Maine have been addressed as "Maniacs." The old postal clerks would read widely, gleaning odd bits of information, hoping to help the mail distribution in so doing. It worked. A letter addressed to The Original Jerkwater Town was delivered. In 1869 the New York Central railroad pioneered a device which enabled locomotives to take on water without stopping. This came to be called jerking water. The first town to have such a system was Montrose, N.Y.

Another word that connotes an obscure town or crossroads is Podunk. Officially, there are no places named Podunk, and an encyclopedia mentions only a tribe of Indians of this name that lived in Connecticut, whose village also bore the name. However no mail addressed only to Podunk has been delivered.

A knowledge of current events was necessary to make some deliveries. In recent years, when a well-known Washington columnist was involved in a publicized lawsuit he got, without a hitch, some mail addressed only S.O.B., Wash., D.C.

The collecting of postal mementos is so diverse that it is a wonder the word *postology* was not invented long ago to cover this wide range. In 1967 a museum in England advertised for collections of old picture postcards. They were attempting to piece together the social history of the Victorian and Edwardian eras and rightfully thought postcards would provide useful information concerning the buildings and scenes which no longer existed.

Not only collectors of mail Americana, but Civil War buffs and coin collectors as well, are looking for the

circular, transparent discs that were used during the
Civil War to convert stamps into a kind of coin. Mercan-
tile firms provided these cases as a means of advertisement. They were used in both North and South when
coins became almost nonexistent.

Quite similar is the hobby of collecting embossed
stamp cases. At the turn of the century ladies carried
their labels in these elegant containers. Every stylish
lady had one in her purse or around her neck. Most had
hinged covers and a metal link on one side for attaching
a chain. Some men wore them as a watch fob. Nowadays
they may be found in junk or antique shops, often un-
recognized.

Finally, some people use stamps as a means of add-
ing color, a conversational item or an exotic flavor to the
decor of their homes or offices. Instead of making a collection and putting it away they derive pleasure from a
discriminating display of selected articles. The stamps
don't have to be rare or costly to be used effectively. Interesting stamps may be glued onto the backs of large,
clear glass ash trays, then covered with felt to give a con-
trasting background. The finished item may be used as
an ash tray, a desk receptacle for paper clips or on a
dresser for cuff links, pins or coins. This handicraft may
be extended to decorating paperweights, wastepaper bas-
kets, lamp shades and other items. These are creative
projects for imaginative youngsters or oldsters and make
personalized, original gifts.

8.   Dog Bites, Bombs and Scorpions

A post office in America is many things to many people. If you happen to live in Beans Corner, U.S.A., you are served by what the city slicker would call a one-horse outfit. Technically, it is an office of the fourth class, the smallest in size of the official categories, located in an obscure village and operated by one man as a part-time job. But it is no less official than the largest in the land. The U.S. flag is authorized and directed to be flown over this post office as well as over the steel and marble ones in New York and San Francisco.

Postmaster Bill Bean knows all of his customers. They were to be correctly referred to as patrons (until March 1971), according to *Postal Laws and Regulations*, the bible of the Post Office. When Bill gets ready to retire, there will be no trouble finding a successor. The receipts of the office may be only several hundred dollars a year, but the pay is several thousand.

I first met this postmaster some thirty years ago, when being an employee of the Post Office Department carried with it a badge of honor and distinction. The United States then had only 250,000 postal employees, handled only one-third of the world's mail and expended only $800 million in a year. The public was just beginning to get annoyed with statistics—and didn't like to think the department was spending as much for postal service each four hours as was spent in an entire year of Washington's administration. But there were only seventy-five government post offices in all thirteen states then.

Then almost any postman could quote facts and figures about his department. He knew that in the first year of operations (1789), $7,510 was taken in and the books were closed with a deficit of $50. He and the public were proud of their postal service before World War II —and that pride increased in 1943 when the Post Office broke into the black to the tune of over a million dollars. What postman today cares, or is even aware that the deficit for 1971 exceeded $1 billion?

Postmaster Bean, of the old school, proudly exhibits the workings of his trade: the *Directory of Post Offices* which lists every one in the United States, the *Directory of International Mail* which lists the postage rates and conditions for mailing to every country in the world, and all his official rubber stamps. When he leaves office, these will be left to his successor.

As fiercely patriotic and loyal to the Post Office as he is, Bill may forget that he once maintained the status of a third-class office with the pay of a full-time job by fraudently claiming revenue from stamps sold to a friend for use in the city and not in Mr. Bean's postal bailiwick. When the friend died, Bill's stamp sales suffered and the office automatically reverted to fourth class.

In the early 1940's, almost everybody with a postal job was quick to admit that he had a good thing. With the best in fringe benefits—retirement, vacation and sick leave—what other job could compare? Almost every postal employee was a career man and a postologist.

Though characterized as a smiling public servant ambling down a sunny, tree-lined street of friends, the postman had been classified in 1929 by the Federal Compensation Commission as holding the most hazardous job in the entire spectrum of federal employment. But not because of weather and dog bites which the public associates with postal hazards. In 1949, a carrier had a bomb in his mail explode, putting out his eyes and ripping his arms off at the elbow. He lived; and his fellow carriers across the country who prayed for his recovery sent $100,000 for his future. All believed in the camaraderie of the corps.

Such items don't make front-page news. That takes an incident like the one in December of 1967. An eleven-alarm fire required 600 firemen and 120 pieces of equipment to limit the destruction of the Morgan Street Post Office Annex in New York City to several million pieces of Christmas mail. This fire was New York City's worst in twenty years and no one will ever know how many lives this loss of mail touched, but the repercussions were negligible. There is a somewhat lackadaisical attitude of the public towards its mail system. Coincidentally—only eight days previously in the same office, an explosion of a homemade bomb mailed in a package had injured eight employees.

The safety of the employee is of more concern than the mail itself. Few people seem to realize that clerks handling in-transit mail in terminals and other processing units are subjected to a wide variety of catastrophic hazards. Besides the fires and bombs, the American soldier's choice of souvenirs gives us the jitters. During the Vietnam war, one-fifth of the packages from that area checked by customs on arrival at San Francisco contained either guns or ammunition. No one can understand why men trained to handle these dangerous items send them through the mails. To say the least it is illegal; and further, it subjects the postal people and the recipients at home to great danger.

Then in addition to the normal accumulation of dust, you have a range of germs and bacteria as wide as the world from which the letters come. And blood and urine samples routinely being sent through the mails for analysis are often broken, subjecting the employees to contamination.

Even the safe postal jobs have their dangers. One never really knows what's in any package. Though snakes are forbidden, regulations do permit certain reptiles and other potentially dangerous animals to be mailed, even poisonous scorpions. And many carriers have opened a mail box to find, either a result of nature or man-made manipulations, a snake staring at them.

But the hazards are not why Bill Bean's brother, a postman in a large city for the past thirty years, is retiring this year; he doesn't like his job anymore. When he began carrying the mails, he was friends with everyone on his route; but that section of the city is now a ghetto where barred doors and shuttered windows are not uncommon. Some carriers today never see their customers; they serve block after block of apartment houses where the mail is dropped into door slots or inserted in wall receptacles in the lobby.

In certain urban areas, twice a month when relief checks are mailed it is necessary to have plainclothes policemen accompany the postmen on their rounds to prevent mugging and robbery. In 1969 a law was passed making it a federal offense to assult a postal employee while on duty.

Where the older Bean once felt warm and wanted in his work, he is now a robot in his job. He stopped carrying the mail and went inside the office as a clerk. But here, too, the trend of increasing depersonalization of mail service affected him. Though automation is rare in the smaller offices, it predominates in the larger ones. Where once every piece of mail was handled by many devoted hands, now a good percentage is moved along by gears, belts and pulleys.

The metallic clickety-clack of the trays of letters being carried to various sorting points by the automated conveyor system is reminiscent of the deafening noise of the factory which Bean rejected in his youth, in favor of postal employment. Now his post office is a production mill. Closed-circuit television and electric eyes add to the unfriendly atmosphere. Once supervision was hardly necessary; today it is increasingly indispensible.

While once Bean felt a kinship with all postal employees, his fellowship is now limited to a handful of old-timers. Those of the past era don't take to the current generation very well. Bean received his training from straight-laced tutors—exacting task-masters of World War I vintage, who themselves had been taught by Spanish-American War vets. Considering this tradition, how can he fraternize with the temporary workers, housewives, students, hippies and anti-poverty program workers who make up a large part of the current postal personnel?

Brother Bean himself has changed with the passing years. He now lacks the manual and mental dexterity to qualify for a higher-level job operating a sophisticated mail-sorting machine or the background to learn how to service the new, complicated electronic equipment. About ten years ago, he had gotten to the point on the seniority ladder where he would have been considered for a supervisory job automatically just as a ruling came out that all supervisory candidates would have to pass a written examination and undergo an evaluation. Somehow or another, he never made the grade.

In an effort to utilize its seasoned employees, his postmaster appointed Bean a member of a temporary survey team of management, labor and union personnel to study mail complaints and delays. In an informal sampling, the senior men were asked to state what, in their opinions, were the greatest boons to the Post Office in the past thirty years. The two top answers: zip code and a 1968 directive which permitted holding packages of letters together with rubber bands, instead of having to tie them with jute twine as had been done for the past hundred years.

The team also established that it often took as long

for a letter to get from the city post office to its nearby airport as from the airport to a destination three thousand miles away. In fact, letters sent to London, Paris, Frankfort and Rome were regularly being received before those mailed at the same time and place to a location only fifty miles away.

Mr. Bean thinks he may live to see the time when large city post offices, as we know them today, are nonexistent. The working of mail could be farmed out to businesses providing labor on contract. To fellows like Bean everything is getting worse. The dogs are even biting more nowadays. About the only things that don't change are the regulations: contraceptives not mailable, nor beverages over 3.2 percent alcohol, nor infernal machines—whatever that means. He realizes that the Post Office still has the job of selling nonpostage stamps for the Fish and Wildlife Service; but he knows they did get rid of the documentary Internal Revenue stamps at the end of 1967. What changes next?

This man is a victim of the generation gap; and his world is as honorable as anyone else's. He relates all present and expected happenings to the past. He remembers how long it took his father to be reconciled to the postman no longer knocking on the door and blowing his whistle when he delivered the mail. But then the local postmaster didn't mind if the practice was informally continued.

Nowadays, in some new subdivisions, door delivery is not even authorized. The mail is dropped at the curb or the patron must pick it up at the post office. This is in keeping with the trend that cut city deliveries from four daily in business districts and two in residential districts to only three or two in the business districts and one at residences.

Where once it was the rule that the postman presented himself only in full, neat uniform, now certain employees are permitted to wear a cap only. Where it was usual for the postman to be a military veteran or an outstanding individual with political influence, now the "postman" may be a student, part-time worker or even a housewife. Where once you could depend on seeing the mailman only in a gold lettered official truck, now he (or she) may pursue the rounds in a fuchsia-colored personal vehicle. Why, sometimes you don't know whether it's the mailman or the welcome wagon at the door!

Clerks at airport mail facilities once took pride in wearing an imposing shield-type badge depicting the federal eagle. Now it's a paper and plastic name card and the old metal badge is a collectors' item. The brass appurtenances, copper fittings and gilt-lettered signs of the city post office have been replaced by a government grey trimmed with melancholy blue. In a modern city office, though, a mini-skirted Miss Zip is in the lobby to answer questions about evermore complicated rules.

The Bean brothers may not be typical employees. No scientific study has ever been made of the average postal person, perhaps because the postal establishment has always been made up of such diverse types. But they all had some characteristics in common. The carrier or clerk of yesteryear was a man with enough social poise not to be repugnant to the patrons. He had enough diligence and application to duty to perform his tasks to the satisfaction of a discriminating public and his superiors. He was trusted by people and loyal to his employer. As today, though the demands of the job might be resented, he must be dedicated to the mission of meeting those demands.

Probably he took the job as a compromise between what he could obtain and what he aspired to. No one ever got wealthy working at a post office. The job has always been in the nature of public service. The average postal employee of the early forties began his employment in his hometown when almost all postal applicants needed political endorsement. Eventually, because of the diversity

of postal operations, he found his niche. Many of the
country boys were lured by the glamor of the cities, and
then would frown at the little country post office. The
city clerk did as much business in a month, or even a
week, as the postmaster of Bean's Corner did in a year.
But he would always concede that mail service had to be
made available to isolated rural areas as well as the
cities.

The concern of the employee for others was the
greatest single factor that made U.S. postal operations a
success. Whenever I contemplate the composite clerk, I
always think of those I knew. The people who had been
raised during the depression and nurtured on patriotism,
pride and hard work made a hard-hitting team.

Only a few months after I went to work in the Post
Office, we had a simple retirement ceremony for one of
the men—a clerk named Barnes. I remember his emotion;
how with tears streaming down his black face, he proclaimed his pride in his job. As far as he was concerned
there was no higher calling than to be entrusted with the
handling of mail. His words meant a lot to me at the time.
This man was not only a postal employee but a graduate
pharmacist. He once had his own little drug store, but at
a time when colored people (as they were then called)
didn't get many prescriptions filled—and when they did,
it was from a white man's store. So he had closed his
pharmacy and went to work for Uncle Sam.

I remember another truly dedicated clerk who made
up a wild concoction including sulphur and sassafras,
and drank it as a tonic in the springtime—to get the lead
out. Also the fellow who used his vacation each year
gathering ramps and ginseng roots in the hills where he
was born. And I can't forget the man who wore an
asafetida bag around his neck to ward off colds or whatever it was he was trying to avoid. Or the clerk who came
in late and rendered this excuse in all sincerity, "Well,

I wasn't really tardy, I just took my coffee break before coming in!" These characters had their place.

More common was the above-average individual who might well have been successful in the professions had the post office not been fortunate to get him. A generation ago, many men, deciding their chosen profession was not really for them, came into postal service. Quite often, the political boss would solicit these people to better serve his constituency.

These men, in their differences, give a true picture of the American postal establishment. To pick out only one and say he was typical would be the same as pointing out one area of postal service to make a blanket appraisal of the entire institution. If a man criticizes the U.S. Postal Service, exactly what is he criticizing?—rural delivery—city delivery—general delivery—COD—special delivery—certified—insured—registered—international—domestic—first class—second class—third class—fourth class—?—surely not them all!

As we consider all of these services and the people who perform them, we find many divergencies. This is necessarily so, for the U.S. Postal Service is truly "of the people, for the people, and by the people."

9.   Calamity Jane Makes the "Bunion Brigade"

The *Postal Bulletin*, the official POD publication issued weekly to all offices, committed a faux pas when it
spotlighted the 476 mentally retarded employees on its
rolls at that time. This information was meant to emphasize the department's compliance with the Employ the
Handicapped program; but it was lifted out of context
and held up for all to see. Every office in the country
figured it had at least one of them!

According to a recent count the Postal Service ranks
first on a list of forty federal agencies as the government's largest employer of retarded workers. It has several thousand and the postmaster general and the president have said they are going to see that more of the
retarded get postal employment. The management tries
to find suitable posts for those with other handicaps too.
The program works for the benefit of all. One of the least
hectic Christmas seasons I spent was when a group of
students from a school for mutes was sent to the post
office where I worked as additional seasonal help. In the
midst of the rush it was really a silent night that Christmas eve.

Eighty percent of the $10 billion postal budget goes
as pay to personnel, who number 750,000, many attracted
by the rewards of Civil Service. They get a minimum of
nine paid holidays each year (Columbus Day was added
in 1971) and thirteen days of sick leave. This is in addition to thirteen days of annual leave each year for a new

employee, twenty days after three years, and twenty-six days after fifteen years of service. Military time or other federal employment counts towards leave category and retirement. Many retired military come into postal service because they start in the maximum leave category. If an employee is a military reservist he may be allowed as much as fifteen days for training or summer encampment. The *Postal Manual* also states that employees "who desire to vote or register in any election or in referendums on a civic matter in their community shall be excused for a reasonable time for the purpose."

In addition to the bountiful fringe benefits such as liberal life, health and accident insurance, they get extra compensation for night, Sunday and holiday work and service performed outside their regularly assigned shift. If snowfall gets too heavy, administrative leave may be granted. They also get official time for certain union activities, and may even be excused to serve as an honor guard at a veteran's funeral. They can go to a local hospital, or Red Cross unit, give a pint of blood and take the rest of the day off.

Judges and lawyers seem partial towards government workers when it comes to selecting juries; and when this duty falls on them, postal workers know they'll lose nothing, not even the extra pay they normally would have gotten for working a night shift. If an employee gets sick on the job, his time at the first-aid room won't normally be charged as leave if he is back to clock out at the end of the shift. If perchance he should die during a work day, he will be credited with working that entire day.

With these benefits, the average gripe is just a healthy blowing-off of steam. For there is a sense of satisfaction in being a link in the postal chain which provides a handclasp around the world. Still, probably every new employee is told by his seniors, "I started out thinking the Post Office had an opening for me. Yeah, I'm in the same hole right now!"

In its early days the Post Office Department was as noted for adherence to a policy of hiring only blue-blooded citizens as it is now known for its policy of nondiscrimination. The second largest nonmilitary employer in the nation (after American Telephone and Telegraph) should set an example. It employs nearly 200,000 members of minority groups including more than 137,000 Negroes, 35,000 Spanish-speaking persons, 1,000 American Indians and 4,000 orientals.

The United States once had a law stating that only free men could be government employees; slavery was not compatable with postal or other government work. Only after the Civil War was the first Negro appointed letter carrier. He was John W. Curry of Washington, D.C.; appointed in 1867. Today the Post Office is the largest employer of Negroes in the nation; and one-fifth of all postal employees are Negro.

In 1961 fewer than ten percent of the managerial positions were held by nonwhites. As of this writing it is about twenty percent; and Negroes head the three largest post offices in the country: New York, Chicago and Los Angeles.

In 1970 the Post Office Department, in an effort to assist minority business enterprise, departed from its traditional policy of depositing its $20 million in daily deposits only in large commercial banks, one to a city, and started placing more than $70 million a year of postal funds in twenty-five black-owned banks throughout the nation.

It is not uncommon to hear certain ethnic groups point out a postal fact of which they in patricular are proud: the word *post* comes from the Latin root *posita*, or the word *letter* originates with the French or some famous person once earned his living by wearing the letter-carrier uniform. Indians know they had brave forefathers who compassionately delivered colonial mail. Eskimos covered long, cold mail routes before they were given citizenship. Today everybody counts when it comes to the U.S. mail.

The uniform of postal employees is worn proudly. Individually, the 235,000 uniformed employees probably value their $125 annual clothing allowance as much for the esprit de corps it contributes as they do for the monetary gain. It is $26 million well spent by the government. After several years of uniform allowance, a man will have a full wardrobe; and then, since he has to present a sales receipt or forfeit the money, he can start buying fifty-dollar shoes. An emolument of the Bunion Brigade.

The U.S. populace has traditionally expected postal employees to appear prim and almost servile in their concern to perform a service to the satisfaction of their patrons. Notice my terminology. It is only a tradition and only an expectation. Today in an age of new-found freedoms, we have to become acclimated to the changing times.

Not long ago, when freedom in male attire first became socially acceptable, the proponents of prudery got a good laugh when the former Post Office personnel chief, Richard J. Murphy, who had set very conservative guidelines for employees' dress, was observed at a party wearing a white Nehru suit, turtle neck sweater and, of all things, beads!

Private business is generally able to cope with such things as odd dress as it sees fit, but the government has to be passive. Although many would feel that uniformed employees could be denied the right to exercise their whimsical desire for flamboyant garb or lack of it—beads and earrings or barefeet and bared bodies—the courts have just about decreed that the federal government, as an employer, not be so square. The invasion of liberalism started in California and spread eastward. Recently the postmaster in Washington, D.C. declared that he would have to look in the personnel records of some employees to determine if they were male or female. Their postal

patrons will have to resign themselves to not knowing
whether they have a postman or a postwoman!

Even those who do not wear a uniform should wear
their status proudly. Every good clerk has a sense of
pride that the word which describes his position was
derived from the ecclesiastical. The church was the center
of learning and the scholars attached to the church were
also designated as *clerical*.

History is full of mentions of men who interested
themselves with mail services. Today's dedicated clerks
are proud to relate themselves to their counterparts of
past generations, especially those described as *scriveners*.
When literacy was at a premium, these men wrote and
read letters for their fellow citizens. Thus, traditionally,
those capable and selected to handle other people's mail
engendered respect.

A favorite pastime of postmen is telling harrowing
tales to illustrate the slogan "The mails must go
through!" Spurred by these traditions of the past, today's
clerks speed the mails and minimize boredom by playing
certain postal games. There is Post Office Bingo. Two or
more clerks sorting letters run a speed race in seeing who
will be the first to find a letter for each of the four corners
of his case, the separations which get the smallest quantities. While speeding production, it also offers amuse-
ment and (though forbidden) possibly a little jackpot to
the winner.

Back in the days when women employees were
rather a rarity in postal service, many offices—the personnel being mainly veterans—could just about staff
their own National Guard unit. But things began to
change. An official study of recruiting postal personnel
in the 1960's showed it took thirteen weeks to hire an
employee and sixty-seven percent of the job applicants
did not complete the process. Regardless, the authorized
slots did get filled—fifteen percent of the time by women.

Since about forty percent of the "weaker sex" in

the United States are now gainfully employed outside of their homes, the "wimmin workers" are recognized as a power to be dealt with. About 107,000 women work for the Postal Service and forty percent of the nation's 32,000 post offices are headed by women.

Several of the top administrative jobs in the Postal Service are being held by women and a woman, Mrs. Virginia Brizendine, once headed the philately division, one of the highest ranking positions at headquarters. Two of the largest post offices in the country: Pasadena, Calif, and Lansing, Mich. have women postmasters. Throughout the United States there are over a hundred female supervisors and nearly two hundred female assistant-postmasters.

Officially women are never referred to as postmistresses. They are postmasters though they be feminine and the word *postmistress* listed in the dictionary. This should gratify the Labor Department's enforcers of equal-rights laws.

Woman's Lib reached the Post Office early. Since Colonial days, women have had postal employment—albeit usually in the more sedate positions. A noted exception was the famous Western character Calamity Jane. (Martha Jane Burke—1852?–1903). She carried U.S. mail under the most hazardous conditions between Custer, Mont. and Deadwood, S. Dak. More routinely, in 1917, three years before women gained the vote, the nation's first female mail carrier, Mrs. Permelia Campbell Whitcomb, started walking her route in Washington, D.C.

But many feel the use of women needs more consideration. A man and a woman are, by law, equal. But when the time comes to handle the sacks of mail, generally it is the man who does it; they claim. Chances are later, if the woman is still around, she will be situated in a comparatively easy job whereas the man avers he will still be asked to load the truck. What is needed is two pay levels: one for clerical duties and another—paying more money—for clerical duties plus ability and willingness to endure prolonged standing and physical work.

Many of the men candidly say that we should operate as they do in Russia where an estimated seventy percent of the postal employees are women and they do most of the physical labor. This may come true yet, because the U.S. Postal Service is one of the largest employers of women in our country; and this is just the beginning. The number has doubled in recent years. If the percentage goes much higher, women will have to load the trucks.

The job of road clerk in the Railway Mail Service (now officially the Mobile Service) has been comparable to a miner's job, as far as a woman is doing it is concerned. But things had to change on the RPO trains too. On November 25, 1966 (remembered as a landmark day by the old boys) a substitute clerk in the Kansas City post office exercised her prerogative, applied and was accepted for an emergency vacant run on St. Louis and Kansas City R.P.O. Train No. 17.

This was the culmination of the efforts of another woman in that office who several years previously had charged discrimination because she was not permitted to make a road run. Naturally, when the grievance finally reached the Bureau of Appeals and Review, it was decided in line with the current, modern outlook that a woman could be placed in such a position if she so chose. After her historic run with no place to change her clothes or a restroom for her use, when queried about the trip, Miss Linda Gardner said, ". . . I won't volunteer again."

Many ladies find postal service very much to their liking. And it is probably easier to get into than the average well-paying job. In 1965 there were 370 women letter carriers. Now there are over 3,500 and about half of all distribution clerks are women. Percentagewise, more women have the job of machine-sorting mail than men. This is attributed to their ability for intense concentration and manual dexterity.

Besides the positive results of the employment of females, there are negative aspects, too. The supervision of a mixed crew will test the ability of a foreman. Often there is contention. The male charges the female talks too much; and the female charges that the male talks too rough. And since their absenteeism is higher, especially during child-bearing years, the productivity of women is limited. The hard-rock men sometimes say they want a firmer organization and that the mail service did not become a morass until so many women entered the work force. But it is suspicioned that, given a choice, they would not revert to the "good old days."

Indicative of the changing times, in December 1971, Mrs. Jane W. Curie, 32, of Ft. Worth, and Janene Gordon, 23, of Sacramento, became the first women postal inspectors when they finished a training course with 22 men.

10.   "Does Mail Move Slower by Donkey or Elephant?"

Thomas Jefferson, in a letter to T. Coxe in 1779, said of politics, "Whenever a man has cast a longing eye on offices, a rottenness begins in his conduct." Thus it was then, so it continued. Americans have justified a host of actions that would ordinarily be anything but proper by in effect saying "to the victor belong the spoils!"

Political patronage had been practiced in the Post Office since our very first days. George Washington, himself, exercised nepotism by giving postal jobs to his in-laws. But patronage became rampant when Andrew Jackson came into office in 1829. He delightedly found the federal government had eleven thousand employees, eight thousand of whom were politically-appointed post-masters. When his postmaster general balked at making so many partisan appointments, the indomitable General Jackson kicked him upstairs to a seat on the Supreme Court and got another lieutenant who would more readily take orders. History calls Jackson the father of patron-age. He saw to it that no man could get, or keep, a job as postmaster unless he was of the dominant political party.

When Lincoln was inaugurated in 1861, he was faced with the problem of patronage. A completely new party was in power and everyone expected all govern-ment jobs to be up for grabs. Lincoln and his postmaster general were literally mobbed by office seekers. Though the dispensing of favors is an ingredient in the balm of glory for victors, an excess of applicants over openings can cause troubles.

Lincoln was fully aware of the pressures patronage brought. Once when abed with a highly communicable disease and the patronage seekers were at his bedroom door, he shouted in disgust, "Let them all in, for now I have something that I can give to everybody!" But his solution to the problem was to establish the patronage system that plagued the Postal Service until its reorganization.

To divert the pressure and scatter the applicants back to their home towns, Lincoln and Blair ordered that postmasterships would be parceled out on recommendations of the local congressmen of their party, and the White House would concur with them all. This was how the mechanics of postal patronage was spelled out. For 108 years it was the procedure by which every postmaster across the nation came into his job.

Ordinarily, the representatives had carte blanche authority to appoint whomever they chose. The senators, who represented entire states, were given the prerogative to select the appointees in their own home towns, but generally took little individual interest in postal appointees. Prior to the ratification of the Seventeenth Amendment to the Constitution, they had little need to build a dynasty based on patronage. Until 1913, they were elected by the members of the state legislatures rather than by popular vote. The senators, however, maintained a certain amount of control over all appointments because in 1836 that body had decided that it was their duty to confirm all presidential appointees.

In 1883 the Pendleton Act created the Civil Service Commission. Although excluding the 47,000 postmasters, it ordered the jobs of clerks and carriers, in any office with as many as fifty employees, filled by means of open competitive exams. Prior to this the postmasters had generally hired and fired their own carriers as they saw fit, which made them the kingpins of postal patronage in their localities. The new law cut away much of the political power of many postmasters. The 1893 regulation that put all clerks and carriers under Civil Service reached the rest.

But patronage continued to be a problem. On March 31, 1917, in an effort to appease the critics of American political practices, President Woodrow Wilson signed an executive order requiring that postmaster appointments—to all offices except the fourth-class ones—be made from open competitive examinations; the appointee had to be one of the three people making the highest score.

Adroitly, the politicians circumvented the intent of this law by advising their preselected candidate to take the qualifying exam and they would take care of the rest. If that man scored in the top three, he was in; if he did not, no one was appointed. Then, a suitable time later, another test would be given, continuing until the congressman's own selection finished in the top three.

It was not until 1928, forty-five years after the clerks and carriers had been put under civil service, that postmasters came under it also. The Ramspect-O'Mahoney Act was thought necessary because each succeeding administration was still removing postmasters for the sole purpose of installing their own in the positions. But that law didn't affect the manner of appointing postmasters; it still allowed the politicians to do that. However it made it very difficult to remove undesirable ones. Once a man got his appointment he was automatically under the cloak of civil-service security.

The late American humorist Will Rogers once said: "I don't make jokes, I just watch the government in Washington and report the facts." His observation is still correct. In 1970, a wag suggested: "Instead of using the Post Office, allow the president to appoint a cabinet level *politmaster* general; and allow congressmen to appoint a *politmaster* instead of a *postmaster* in every town in the nation. Then postal operations could be put into the hands of those who operate them."

Politics was practiced not only to get and retain postal positions. After entering the office, the apprentice became part of a political program. It was inescapable in the scheme of things that politics was practiced by unions and other lobbyists to effect legislation. On an individual basis political influence was brought about by whoever could and would. Naturally the members of Congress were expected to provide a lot of influence and often they exhibited the ethics of hypocritical religious zealots.

An example of how some government employees have graciously accepted their desserts, was shown once when the House of Representatives was discussing legislation that would give them more benefits. Congressman Passman of Louisiana, reflecting the mood of the House, arose and said: "I rise in opposition to the bill; but I certainly hope it passes!"

Federal employees have been politically courted because these three million workers and their families amount to over six million votes. In addition to the always-available free help from up-and-coming politicians, postal people have had working for them some of the best professional politicians that money could buy. These politicians stayed aware of the possibilities for action. This was their job. They knew what positions could be filled directly by appointment. They knew what others required qualifying periods of experience, some as much as five years. So it was not uncommon for a man to take a clerical position he wouldn't ordinarily accept if he realized that in time he would be pushed up.

Circuitous routes were sometimes taken to achieve the purpose. I remember a man who wanted to be postmaster of his home town and knew the incumbent would soon be ready to retire. There was no problem about his

standing with the local political party, but his representative had publicly avowed to appoint only career employees
as postmasters and rural carriers. Furthermore, there
was no local vacancy at any level nor any contemplated.
But this proved no deterrent to a good politican.

His congressman, whose bailiwick encompassed
sixty or so postmasterships, showed him how to plan. The
aspirant got a job in the post office of a nearby metropolitan area and commuted each day, retaining his home
as before. When the old postmaster retired, his congressman simply had the aspirant transferred back to his home
town. Thus the congressman had fulfilled his promise of
impartiality, and at the same time had favored a particular constituent in the best political tradition. Somewhere between truth and falsehood is something called
smart politics. Since July of 1970, congressmen are supposed to be out of postal politics; and for several years
prior to that the Hatch Act restricted government employees from currying favors from the congressmen, but
no legislation can present a politician or postman from
being smart.

Personnel appointments made under the spoils system many times caused anguished outcries. In 1881
President Garfield was shot by a disappointed office
seeker and the public had then clamored for a law to take
government employee appointments away from the politicians. They reasoned that President Garfield was a
mortal victim of the spoils system. This same clamor
brought about the latest postal reform.

On February 5, 1969, a new president—Richard
Nixon—announced that he was indeed going to fulfill a
campaign promise by proposing legislation to end the
need for Senate approval of postmasters and to allow
selections to be made by the postmaster general. Thus we
reverted to the position from which President Lincoln
and PMG Blair sought to divest themselves. Except, of
course, it was taken for granted that as a general rule

promotions would be made from the ranks of employees already on the Post Office rolls.

When Nixon made his statement, he was trespassing in an area many congressmen wanted to keep their domain. Some 3,400 postmasters and rural carriers, each with a political sponsor, were appointed in an average year. President Johnson had asked for the same legislation, but had not pushed for it. President Nixon will be remembered as a man with the courage to break with a tradition upheld by the previous thirty presidents. However, he made the changes only after putting his own men in the top departmental jobs and as directors of the fifteen postal regions.

Coupled with the proposal to operate the post as a semi-corporate body, not under the direct control of Congress, the changes prompted James H. Rademacher, president of the National Association of Letter Carriers, to warn that "a ruthless and cynical postmaster general could become the most powerful dispenser of patronage in the nation."

Virtually every new postmaster general, upon taking office, had expressed amazement and disgust at the workings of the bureaucracy of which he assumed control. When Winton Blount took office in 1969 he found a section in his headquarters whose sole job was to respond to inquiries from Capitol Hill and other citadels of politics regarding postmaster and rural-carrier appointments. He indicated shock that sixty-four people were assigned to this job and said: "As far as I'm concerned, they don't need three."

In spite of verbal assaults against loss of patronage, many congressmen seemed relieved they no longer had to endorse postal job applicants. This had always made enemies of the several unsuccessful contenders for every job, and only one friend. Since the postal patronage plums had of late ofttimes been snickered at in terms of pay and prestige, some rather agreed with Sen. Gale

McGee's suggestion that the party which *lost* the election should be saddled with the burden of filling these jobs.

Amongst the reasons submitted on behalf of continuing the practice of letting congressmen decide who would be appointed postmasters, one stood out. If the Post Office were a completely closed organization, restricting postmaster appointments to employees already having career status, many employees would be promoted to jobs above their qualifications. Thomas P. Costin, Jr., president of the National Association of Postmasters made the point quite well. He held that a postmaster needed to be an experienced civic-minded leader. The man selected was more important than the method used. The postmasters association, aware that two-thirds of their number were appointed from outside the postal ranks, was willing to keep it that way.

The association felt that a man who had come up through the ranks would have spent practically all of his working years tied to the confining requirements of a clerical job; and might not have had the administrative and civic experience desirable in a postmaster. The traditional procedure insured the selection of the best man available. They were implying, as discreetly as possible, that career postal employees lacked the broader experience available to people in other positions.

When it was obvious the new administration was going to change the procedure of selecting postmasters and opponents could do nothing about it, the National Association of Postmasters, in a politically-wise decision, joined with the National League of Postmasters and reversed their position. The association's president, representing ninety percent of the nation's 32,000 postmasters, went on record as saying the new procedure was a "tremendous step forward to help insure the selection of the best qualified man . . ." These differing opinions tended to underline a sentence in the report of President Johnson's Commission on Postal Organization which recommended that the Post Office Department be scrapped. "In appearance, many people are responsible for running the Post Office. In fact, no one is."

Viewed on a national scale, the huge map of the United States shows thousands of towns and cities, each with its own postmaster. Each of these postmasterships had been a feudal fief. The postmaster had been appointed by virtue of his politics. Purely and simply. Chances were that he would spend the rest of his life in that position. He wore a badge of honor because he had proven his mettle within his environs. No one can argue with success; and this man was successful—he was postmaster. The system was so traditional that no one questioned it. For generations every town in America had at least one of these well-paying jobs that the ruling clique could give to one of their party. Typically, the PM, as he was sometimes called, had been more interested in carrying the precinct than the mail.

Looking closer at the map, visualize a small geographic area in an highly industrialized and densely populated part of our country; an area about thirty miles in each direction, not too big for one individual to know intimately. Within this area where often one good man could have done the entire managerial job, there were eight or so different postmasters: two good, two bad and four indifferent. The two good ones spent a large portion of their time beating their heads against the wall, trying to develop some communication within their areas. The bad ones couldn't have cared less. "After all, what's an assistant for? Besides, I've got a lot of civic duties!" The four indifferent ones plodded along with an assist here and there from the regional and departmental officers who kept a check on their offices.

Though the efficiency of the clerks and carriers and their successive levels of managers could be directly linked to their morale and measured at any time by their enthusiasm, the efficiency of the postmaster general was never questioned. He had always been a political appointee. His chief qualifications? Having helped the national party to an extent befitting this reward that could be used as a springboard for further advances. The office of the postmaster general was often a position from which a political administrator could secure the necessary national background for an international job.

Every new PMG, upon taking office, had announced that he was going to improve the service, but he usually was strictly a politician, not a professional manager. Further, his average length of service was less than three years, an insufficient period to qualify him as being a proficient postal manager at even the expiration of his tenure.

For the most part, the postmaster generals' hands were tied, and when not tied, they seemed to be sitting on them. Consequently few made any startling changes. Basically until the reform, the job was as it was at its inception, hardly more than a figurehead for the establishment.

But it was not only PMG's and their postmasters who came into being at the behest of politics. Rural carriers, even though they were civil-service employees, got their jobs through patronage. Seldom was an opening filled without several men contending for it, and seldom, if ever, was an appointment made to one with no political pull. Rural carrier appointments were controlled even though they did not require congressional action and a presidential signature. Generally, the applicants were cleared through the local executive committee of the political party in power. It, of course, had a direct line to their own member of the House of Representatives.

The job of a rural mail carrier had always been considered as one of the most desirable in the mail service. In most respects it is a position separate and apart from all others, and the employees are generally considered within their offices to be their own boss. The politically

selected rural carrier often stepped into a job that paid
more money than was being received by clerks and carriers working in the same office for twenty or more years.
In the small third or fourth-class offices they might be
paid as much or more than the postmaster himself. Their
pay is determined by a formula that includes such factors
as number of boxes served. In addition to the basic pay a
mileage allowance is added for the use of personal vehicles on the nearly two million miles of travel the rural
carrier business requires each day.

All of these advantages often made them—if they
had a mind to be—very independent of their nominal
boss, the postmaster. Rural carriers were wont to say:
"To hell with the postmaster, Representative X gave me
my job, the same as he gave him his. I know where I
stand!"

Whenever musing on the vagaries of postal personnel, I think of how the Post Office is enmeshed with other
elements of our society. Post Office officials often provide
unique and necessary services. One instance is when a
town wants to change its name. The mayor might present
the name that had been selected only to find that such a
change is controlled by the Board on Geographic Names
under the Department of the Interior. No place may
change its official name without the acquiescence of this
federal body. But probably the most effective endorsement would be a write-up of the rationale for change by
the postmaster. So postal officials, like doctors, lawyers
and fire chiefs, are nice to have around when needed.

For that reason being a postal official has always
commanded respect. In an always-changing America, it
was inevitable that these public servants would get
caught in the maelstrom of evolution. The concept of
their selection was on a parity with the times.

Students of postal history now see progress. Eighty
years ago, the postmaster of Coshocton, Mass. was in
jail because he didn't deliver the letter of appointment

to his successor; and the new postmaster of Norwich, Conn. fired all his Democratic letter carriers, and replaced them with Republicans.

Hopefully there is no longer need for rough-riding actions from the Civil Service Commission. In that job in 1889 Theodore Roosevelt stormed into Troy, N.Y., to get at the postmaster who had fired every one of his Democratic carriers and hired Republicans. Teddy knew that postal employees—whether equated to donkeys or elephants—were still human.

11. $3 Million Spent on a $1.5 Million Theft!

Everyone is familiar with the token of appreciation proffered at Yuletide to the milkman, handyman, postman, etc. This is in keeping with the spirit of the occasion. And people see nothing drastically wrong in the junior mail carriers getting the least preferred routes while the senior man chooses a more affluent area. But the postal employee has to be careful that gratuities are not extended into the realm of payoffs that border on bribery. Specifically, some minor officials accept, and come to expect, an annual gift from those with whom the Post Office does business.

The donor of the gift could be an airlines station manager and the postal official the recipient of a minimum gift—some liquor. But there are a dozen airlines serving the city, so he gets one from each, or his annual supply of booze. Anytime a government employee accepts gifts for which official consideration is expected in return, he leaves himself wide open for criticism.

Something is not given for nothing. Public carriers of the mails, i.e.: trains, trucks, busses, airlines, etc., can be fined for wilful or negligent mishandling of the mail. This is a common occurence whereby a prescribed part of the company's pay is forfeited, as decreed by federal statutes, whenever they cause delay or damage to the mails. The write-ups of these events can very easily be killed by certain officials. No one knows how many such fines have been settled under the table with a bottle.

Conversely, a lot of criticism of the mails is completely unwarranted. People point to the date on a postage tape and smirk, "See the carriers are delivering letters before the postmark shows they were mailed. That's one way to get fast delivery!" In fact, the mailer had a private postage meter and set it for an incorrect date. The validity attached to an official postmark is the subject of ample rules and regulations. It may be used in a court of law to verify the time of an event.

To determine whether the postage tape was applied by a post office or a private postage mailer look closely at the lower part of the American eagle. A very small *P* to the left and an *O* to the right denote official application. If there are, instead, other letters the postage was applied privately by a person who purchased or rented the machine; P.B. means the machine was manufactured by Pitney-Bowes. These machines are taken to the local post office to pay for the dispensable postage tape.

Patron-held tape machines are easy "stamp sales" and credited to the post office to which the meter is assigned. Because the postmaster's pay, and in certain cases the pay of his clerks, is determined in part by the sales of the offices, the *U.S. Code*, Title 18, Section 1712, headed "Falsification of Postal Records to Increase Compensation," specifically forbids postmasters to take credit for the stamp sales not meeting certain requirements. Part 322 of the *Postal Manual*, the post office Bible, details unallowable sales. Since not only do sales help salaries, but enough can move a post office into the next higher category, many see this system as engendering dishonesty, and maintain that even when honestly administered it is not an equitable way of setting pay scales. No doubt the situation will someday be changed, and these details just another chapter in postal history.

Illegal practices by some Post Office employees are nothing new. A hundred years ago, P. H. Woodward, in his popular book, *Guarding the Mails*, drew upon his service as chief special agent under PMG Jewell. He wrote that of 410 arrests made the year ending April 30, 1876, 162 of them were of postal officials.

But postal employees do not have a monopoly on questionable practices; often their patrons are as quilty. Specifically, I refer to short-paid mail. An enterprising person in charge of a mailroom can generally manage to save his company a lot of money—enough to warrant a big, juicy bonus. The large, publicly held corporations provide no incentive towards short payment of postage. It's the small businesses, individuals or the family-held companies that do it.

They know from experience that a package with a bunch of stamps on it will probably get through. Few postal clerks take the trouble to add them all up. Also, there's a postal regulation which states if apparently a stamp has fallen off an article, it shall be assumed to have had the correct postage. Another regulation states no systematic search shall be made for short-paid articles. A lot of private mailers know more about this sort of thing than many of the postal clerks.

In airmail going out of the country, exchange office clerks are expressly forbidden to "rate" a letter no more than two cents short or a parcel no more than twenty-five cents short. This makes sense. The Post Office couldn't break even collecting a few pennies, but this stipulation allows patrons to pay less than they should, repeatedly. In 1967 when the foreign airmail card rate went from eleven cents to thirteen cents, few knew of the increase and the department was lax in publicizing it. So generally the public paid two cents short and nothing could be done about it. Likewise the postage increases in 1971 prompted minor deficiencies with some foreign destination mail that were non-collectible by the Post Office.

To many mailers, short payment is a calculated risk. And the mailer wins in the long run—if moral qualms don't bother. Except for foreign mail sent on to its destination, there's no penalty if one is caught. He must only pay the short postage.

Although normally post offices are not very good places for an outsider to rob, the biggest cash robbery in U.S. history was not from a bank or Brinks. It was the $1.5 million mail robbery in Plymouth, Mass. in 1962. When the federal statute of limitations expired on Aug. 14, 1967, the government acknowledged that it had spent more money on the investigation than was taken in the robbery. A century in man-years had been spent on the case and the only indicted suspects were acquitted. In the early days of our nation's history, conviction of mail robbery carried a death penalty. If the Plymouth robbers had been caught and successfully prosecuted, the only penalty would have been a fine, prison sentence and the stigma of society.

The nation's postal service, like its military, has always symbolized the bulwark and might of the federal government. In the forefront, leading and maintaining this most admirable record (the preceeding paragraph notwithstanding) is its law enforcement arm—the Postal Inspection Service. These employees do everything from auditing postal accounts to maintain employee honesty to the apprehension of mail thieves. In the case of the big-city riots in 1967, when transportation was at a standstill, inspectors were even used to maintain a twenty-four watch and transport and help the presidentially-appointed investigating committeemen.

In addition to covering the activities within America, postal inspectors may be faced with international incidents. The U.S. Mail has not been disregarded in modern criminal activities. Organized crime now directs many postal violations. Money orders are counterfeited wholesale in such places as the Philippine Islands.

A recent annual report shows over 15,000 Postal Inspection arrests for everything from mailing poisons to holdups, fraud and extortion. Mail theft is punishable by a two thousand dollar fine and a five-year jail term but the courts have been loath to exact this maximum upon offenders. Indicative of the hopelessness of the times is the postmaster general's report which stated: "In the past year postal inspectors arrested for the third time Harvey A. Dart, for stealing checks from the mail." Altogether, he had negotiated more than forty thousand dollars in stolen checks. Page 33 of the *1968 report* tells of a man who, in the two-year period prior to his apprehension, had stolen and negotiated over $250,000 in checks. The preceding page tells of an offender who had a record of at least *twelve arrests* for stealing from mail receptacles over a thirty year period. And in the latter part of 1971 a man appeared before a Senate investigating committee claiming to have stolen more than $1 million worth of mail at various airports!

The work performed by the postal inspectors gives a good insight into the present-day post office. In fiscal 1965, the year-end tally showed 533 postal employees arrested for theft. The department thought things couldn't possibly get worse; but the figure climbed steadily each year and now is more than double that. The small offices have less thievery; but any is too much.

All losses cannot be attributed to in-house theft. In 1969, burglary and losses in postage stamps and cash from 1,929 offices amounted to over $3 million, at that time the heaviest loss for any year in history. There were 131 holdups compared to 82 in the preceding year. A total of 123,574 blank money-order forms were stolen and 3,848 of these were subsequently cashed. The number of arrests for mail thefts from private and apartment receptacles and possession of stolen mail totaled 6,487, also the highest number to that time.

In addition there were 1,489 investigations involving firearms and bombs. One of these, a ten-month investigation, netted a life sentence for a man in Cleveland, Ohio who mailed an explosive device which instantly killed the addressee, his rival in a romantic affair. And inspectors effected 527 arrests involving narcotics and dangerous drugs in postal-related cases.

After a two-year investigation, four professional burglars were arrested in the Bronx and $50,000 in stamps and four bags of registered mail including $3 million in securities was recovered. Two thieves were caught at O'Hare airport in Chicago after stealing mail containing an estimated $2 million. Four men were arrested in New York City on their way to perforate four million counterfeit stamps. They were offering them at a quarter of face value. The 15,150 arrests in 1969 was another record. And 98 percent of those brought to trial were convicted—a total of 11,472.

Perhaps this was the year that prompted the joke about the mail carrier charged with theft. When the judge asked, "Why did you steal this mail?", he answered, "I didn't steal it, I just carried it home for a joke." Fined $250, the indignant defendant demanded, "What's that for?" "That," said the judge, "is for carrying a joke too far!"

Citizens may claim as much as $3,000 reward for helping postal inspectors catch those who rob post offices, mail bombs or send poison or other dangerous materials through the mail for other than legal reasons. For burglary, theft of mail, forgery and the like, a $300 reward is paid to anyone who gives the necessary information.

Many post offices have a lookout system built into the walls of the buildings. These observation platforms feature a false partition. An inspector may enter a catwalk behind the partition from the outside of the building, unknown to the employees inside. There he can observe them through one-way glass as they perform their duties. The inspectors are sometimes referred to as the Barefoot Brigade, because they might take off their shoes to enter the galleries more quietly.

This set-up, expensive to build and maintain, was started in 1892 in Cincinnati and the department became so enamored of it, it was made nationwide. Its effectiveness cannot be denied. Besides its practical aspects, it is a psychological deterrent to stealing for the employee to know that his actions may be observed. However, the law enforcement arm of postal management has had no desire to draw public attention to this part of their system.

In 1966 when Gronouski became postmaster general, he ordered the glass looking into the men's toilets covered up. His rationale was that women employees were not observed in their toilets, so to watch only the men was discrimination. The Inspection Service put up a howl, rightfully maintaining their best efforts would go down the drain. In the privacy of a restroom, employees could open a letter, take the money out of it and flush the evidence down the commode.

Until recently, the Inspection Service accepted no candidate more than thirty-nine years of age. This was unrealistic when compounded by another requirement that the man must have five years of postal experience. Quite often, by the time an interested employee served his five years, he was overage for the promotion. Both rules were made in a generation when the inspectors had to ride horseback and fight train robbers; life expectancy and geriatrical productivity were far less than today. But this is past history. The Postal Service is now putting the emphasis on efficiency, not tradition. Applicants no longer need prior postal experience. Educational requirements have been established with the minimum a high-school diploma, though most appointees have a college degree.

The Inspection Service, now numbering about 1,400,

has suffered its share of brickbats, too. It was started as
the elite of the old Post Office Department and continues
a select body of the new Postal Service. Probably the
major question on the application, until recently, was
the candidate's political affiliation. This was necessary
because the Inspection Service, the oldest law enforcement body in our government, was set up to have its
total membership divided between the two major political
parties. This may be traced to the old English custom of
appointing two persons to head a governing unit. In
theory they provided a balance of power and a check on
each other—the same as our two bodies of Congress.

There was an element of judiciousness in extending
the idea to postal services; but in actual practice, it didn't
work as planned. At every change of political power, the
incoming party would tend to appoint only their own
particular political faith and justify their actions as
bringing the balance, shifted by the predecessor party,
back in line.

Maintaining postal honesty is a job of many faces.
One type of dishonesty that is gaining popularity—with
crooks, not clerks—is to take a ten or twenty dollar
counterfeit bill to the post office and exchange it for
genuine stamps and change. If the clerk can't prove that
he was not properly informed of bogus bills in the area,
he will have to make restitution for his laxity. In a recent
year the department paid for 882 cases where the employee was duped. The rest (how many not known) had
to pay out of their own pocket. It's a time-consuming
chore, and ofttimes an embarrassing one, for a window
clerk to examine a bill for authenticity, especially when
he has customers waiting.

The trouble with our postal organization is that
some things should be cut out but others should be left in,
and too often the professed proficiency experts get confused between the two. Take registered mail, for in-

stance. It was started as a means for the patron to obtain
security for valuable articles by paying an added fee.
Regular insured mail provided indemnity in case of loss
but no extra security precautions were observed in its
handling. Registered mail was to be accorded the maximum in postal security. Originally each time a registered
article was transferred, the handler recorded its number
and had another postal employee witness the act and
certify to it with his signature. This is what is meant by
registering, to keep a record. Now when a registered
article is missing the patron sometimes finds there is no
way to trace it because nominal value articles are often
bulked, the articles simply counted in total quantity, and
the dispatching or receiving clerk need not have a witness
to verify the count. Every step backwards leads to the
ultimate fall. Maybe the relaxed vigil is why one set of
thieves got away with $1.5 million.

In recent years many have seen the Post Office as a
haven for criminals. Epecially when a postal supervisor
was murdered on the job by an employee with a lengthy
criminal record who in years past would not have even
been able to take the entrance exam. This brings us to
the crux of the matter. Much paper and a lot of federal
funds have been used to formulate codes of ethical conduct for government employees. Generally they are over
loaded with flowery words and noble sounding statements.
The department set one forth, so did the Civil Service
Commission, the Congress of the United States and even
the president himself.

They have made for a lot of dull and uninteresting
reading and were generally composed, published and then
forgotten. What we need are old-fashioned commonsense
and common-decency codes. Scrap all the rest and give me
just three excerpts from the ten point Concurrent Resolu-
tion 175, of the House of Representatives in the second
session of the 85th Congress:

"Give a full day's labor for a full day's pay; . . ."

"Seek to find and employ more efficient and economical ways . . ."

"Expose corruption wherever discovered."

Only a few postal employees do not know that honesty is its own reward.

12. No Benefits on a Silver Platter

We are living in a day when the squeaking hinge is the one that gets the oil. Only those who protest are recognized; thus the need for vociferous organizations. And these we have. At the time of the great postal changeover in 1971, eighty-seven percent of all postal employees belonged to unions having the exclusive right to represent their members with management.

There were, at this time, several major postal employee unions, ranging in size from the Letter Carriers—organized in 1889, with more than 200,000 members representing every state in the Union as well as the District of Columbia, Puerto Rico, and the Virgin Islands—to the comparatively small National Association of Postal Supervisors—having about 35,000 members. I emphasize—35,000 was relatively small.

There had been talk for a number of years about a merger of postal unions. Then, in line with the other sweeping changes in 1971, various postal unions began to vote for merger, creating what was to become one of the largest unions of government workers in the entire world.

Of the nearly three million civilian employees in the federal government in 1971, the Post Office had about one-fourth—close to 750,000 workers in more than 44,000 facilities. Since eighty-five percent of them were in the five lowest pay grades and eighty percent would probably finish their careers at the same level they

started, it stood to reason that they would be well un-
ionized. Every single member contributed to the economic might of his union. Altogether, government employees had been paying union dues in excess of $30
million annually.

Though this monetary might is great, there are other
powerful factors to unionization. The Hatch Act prevents
individual employees from campaigning for a partisan
political candidate, but it cannot touch the so-called ladies
auxiliaries. Even so, they too, were only a small part of
the big, open secret.

Much of the success of the unions had to be attributed to leadership. Many of the postal unions' aggressive leaders received their labor education in the days
when being good with your fists might come in handy,
when the unions elected single leaders because married
men couldn't afford the risk of being fired. These old
boys were tough. They played hard ball and they played
for keeps.

The individual unions collectivized. A good example
is the Government Employees Council, a group of thirty-
four unions which represented more than a million federal workers. In February 1969 they voted unanimously
to oppose turning the Post Office Department into a corporation. Not even the federal government could afford
to sell short an ultimatum with so much might and money
backing it.

The *Congressional Quarterly* listed the National Association of Letter Carriers as the biggest lobbyist on
Capitol Hill in 1969; it spent $295,970. The United Fed-
eration of Postal Clerks was in second place spending
$250,827. And it is an honor on Capitol Hill to be known
as the biggest spender in the field of lobbying!

For their half-million dollars, the unions laid claim
to winning $750 million worth of raises for the employees
they represented. A Washington columnist quoted the
Postal Clerks' legislative director as saying: "We get

none of these benefits, such as pay raises and fringe benefits, handed to us on a silver platter. To influence Congress, we have to spend lots of money."

Hopefully, 1970 was the last year of such necessity.
The postal reform law took the wage-setting authority
away from Congress and empowered the new government agency to negotiate wages with the employee
unions.

Previously all legislation had hinged on the major
word: Money! Unions were known to have plenty of that
—especially if it was to be spent on legislation or financ-
ing political campaigns. Political analysts have stated
that unions would gladly give a hundred thousand dollars to a candidate's treasury if it would help the union's
causes. It is a matter of public record that in 1966
Jimmy Morrison of Louisiana spent close to $275,000 in
his unsuccessful race for Congress—and most of it came
from the letter carriers' and clerks' unions!

In fiscal year 1969 the Post Office Department paid
directly to unions almost $14.5 million from dues checkoff
of employees salaries. And the thirteen unions that represented postal employees so well never had to spend any
of their money on strike subsistence funds as was necessary for other unions.

The power of the organized postal employees may be
somewhat appreciated by considering that in November
of 1968 James H. Rademacher threatened that the AFL-
CIO Letter Carriers would claim the right to strike if a
federal corporation took over the mails "on a self-supporting basis." This, in spite of federal employees not
being allowed to strike. His remarks created quite a stir
across the nation, but most people thought he was only
fighting fire with fire. The same threat is made whenever
there is talk of putting the postal union under the Lan-
drum-Griffin Act which requires unions to make public
disclosures of their finances. To date the act exempts federal employee unions, who are quick to retort that if simi-

larly restricted they want the private citizens' rights
too. Namely, the right to strike. Remembering thread-
bare union leaders fighting to have industry's financial
books opened for their inspection, many feel the unions
are now basking in the luxury they once resented. As
Voltaire wrote, "People have declaimed against luxury
for 2,000 years, in verse and prose, and people have always delighted in it."

Over a half million rank-and-file postal workers attribute any job luxury they have to their unions. And the
unions have their rightful place in our society. However,
too often in the past, this place was to fill a void created
by inadequacies in the governmental structure. Typically, postal employees learned of new legislation vitally
affecting them only from the press and union periodicals.
Quite naturally, union information was slanted. Perhaps
one reason why postal unions continuously demanded a
measure of recognition for a job well done is they never
forget the fate of the ancient messenger who was given a
gold coin when he brought the king good news; but upon
bringing the monarch bad news, was beheaded.

Almost every year in Washington, there had been
the drive for a new bill to benefit government workers. It
was always spearheaded by the aggressive postal unions.
Once when the National Association of Letter Carriers
was pushing for a full pay grade increase for its carriers, the leaders of other groups or crafts wondered why
a bigger pay raise should be even considered for letter
carriers alone, since other jobs were as demanding. After
it was all over, it was seen that the letter carriers' union
had gotten *all* postal employees a pay-grade increase!

The carriers always have had a lot going for them.
They settle for only the best and most aggressive union
leaders, smart enough to hire legislative consultants
(lobbyists) welcome to walk into places where others
can't even get an appointment. Also, postal employees
have a daily face-to-face meeting with the public; and

every good postal worker has been indoctrinated with the
need for patron goodwill, which, of course, would stand
him in good stead when he needs it.

Postal workings on Capitol Hill may be deduced by
considering that one fine morning Jerome Keating, then
president of the AFL-CIO Letter Carriers' Union, met at
a closed breakfast affair with all members of a Subcommittee of the House Post Office and Civil Service Commit-
wasn't invited. After the meeting, Keating—to show who
wielded the power—went to Udall's office and proclaimed
to the chairman that his own subcommittee was going to
approve the union's bill. The response to incidents like
this range from an enthusiastic "Congratulations!" to a
cynical "Like a game of marbles, it has to be played on
dirt!"

Postal unionization was inevitable. It was often the
only recourse for the rank-and-file employee. And he
could depend upon it to open the doors for redress. The
unions provided an *esprit de corps* which management
had neglected. Unionization was the cohesive force which
assured the public that their postman would always be as
described by Dr. Charles W. Eliot, the "messenger of
sympathy and love, servant of parted friends, consoler of
the lonely, bond of the scattered family, enlarger of the
common life, carrier of news and knowledge, instrument
of trade and industry, promoter of mutual acquaintance,
of peace and good will among men and nations."

13.   "You Can't Ruin This Country With Politics!"

The general public has never regarded the Post Office as exciting or salted with the flamboyant personalities other government agencies have had. The postal part of the federalcy has had some colorful characters, but these horse-opera actors have been unlike those of the glamor agencies.

The Post Office operates on the reverse of the Hollywood theory that any publicity is good publicity. Its employees don't care to attract attention. Their suavity and reticence amount to what is known as political expertise.

In the closing days of the Johnson Administration, the general counsel of the Post Office announced a change —henceforth it would be departmental policy not to police Congressional use of the free-mailing privilege. With the quietly stated reasons that "The use of franking privileges for correspondence on official business is a matter strictly between the member of Congress and his conscience," the department avoided a great many headaches as well as the collection of money from many congressmen. Notable among those with a tab pending was one senator against whom there was a claim for more than $25,000 in postage for a newsletter mailed to 500,-000 constituents two years previously.

The Post Office claimed, until the reversal of policy, that one section of that newsletter dealt with the senator's election campaign rather than official business. The senator claimed that he had been billed as a form of political harrassment because he had blocked the nomination of Justice Abe Fortas as chief justice of the United States. In this potentially explosive situation the Post Office's political expertise called for political expedience.

Actually, Congress was inextricably entwined with postal operations and the liaison between the two was generally predicated only by a matter of morality. The ethics of Congress always paralleled that of the Post Office. In 1969 (one year before postal reform) the Senate passed the first code of conduct for its members; and it allowed such things as the acceptance of contributions to help defray costs of holding office, travel to and from home states, phone calls, stationery, telegrams, radio-TV reports to constituents, etc.

This law, passed as an aftermath of the censure of Thomas Dodd, required senators to file annual reports with the senate secretary, listing contributions received and speaking fees (honorariums) if the fee exceeded $300. There's apparently no great objection to these men adding to their $42,500 plus salary—assuming the fees are really given for speeches and not as a cover for something else. Under this same law, other income, property, gifts, debts and tax returns may be kept secret unless the Senate Ethics Committee by majority vote considers a senator's conduct under serious question. Senator Aiken's opinion of the law, as passed, was the "farce of the year."

There is a federal law that requires all interstate political committees to report their receipts and expenditures to the Clerk of the House of Representatives. These reports are open for public inspection and the *Congressional Quarterly* makes an annual inspection of these campaign-spending reports. Typically, the organizations have the word *political* somewhere in their names—generally Political Action or Political Education. Some have cover-up names to mask their true identity. Their common denominator is providing money to get the politicians elected. It is ironic that Americans, so quick to

point a derisive finger at social and political practices of
foreign countries, could have been so blasé about their
own country's political philosophy whose purveyors dis-
pensed favors under a *quid pro quo* system.

Rep. Arnold Olsen felt that Congress had a right to
know what the Kappel Commission did with the more
than $1 million it spent in preparing the corporation-
plan report. But other congressmen backscratchingly
opined that this was an executive branch appointment
and there was no accountability to the legislative branch.
Some might have said, "Isn't that what capitalistic
money is for—promoting your own product?" Others
watching the Congressional-postal liaison might have
felt that social democracy is always better at giving people money than teaching them how to use it.

Fortunes have always been found in political hay-
stacks. Those in power have always made hay of their
proposals to engender favor, knowing that when the lobbyists got through with the politicians, the original bills
could not be recognizable. Money has always talked!

Then again, one has to know when to clam up. Sometimes silence is golden. I am reminded of the preacher
who was persuaded to run for Congress on a platform
opposing lobbies. His rascally opponent never said a thing
until the last minute. Then he averred that Washington
was no fit place for a gullible, naive churchman; they
ought to elect an old reprobate so their consciences
wouldn't hurt them for throwing a lamb to those wolves.
The reprobate won! Therefore, the practices which naive,
would-be congressmen oppose, continue.

Intense lobbying preceded a bill to increase postal
employees' pay and the public's postage rates. Senator
Mike Monroney, chairman of the Post Office and Civil
Service Committee, termed some of the tactics employed
by mail lobbyist as odious and the "most vicious it has
been my experience to witness in some twenty-nine years
in Congress." He told the Senate further: "Their type

of lobbying and the morality of their lobbying, I think, leaves one of the blackest marks on the lobby echelon of any national trade association."

In the past forty years the nation's population increased by two-thirds, but the mail volume tripled and this growth was accompanied by unresolved problems. Eighty percent of our mail volume had come to be generated by business institutions, almost all of which belonged to an association dedicated to lobbying for their own special interests. They were unconcerned that the Post Office hadn't operated in the black since 1945 and the postal deficit ran in excess of a billion dollars per year.

In the House, Ken Hechler observed third-class lobbyists "rough, ruthless, cynical." He claimed one of his constituents was offered a political war chest of $100,000 if he would oppose Hechler in a forthcoming election. He felt this showed the length to which the third-class mail lobby would go "to buy a seat in Congress."

Lobbyists have been known to write the bills introduced by certain congressmen. The congressmen need grist for the mills that turn out their images. They can't be expected to know the ins and outs, facts and figures and history and outlook for everything that they talk about, so they use lobbyists (who prefer to be called legislative consultants) to do the writing and to come up with something palatable to all concerned. The renowned J. Don Kerlin is recognized as an authority on postal legislation. He has been employed on occasion by such concerns as the Third-Class Mailers, Time, Inc. and Reuben H. Donnelley Corp. Although a questionable practice, the House Post Office and Civil Service Committee apparently had no qualms about hiring consultants who at the same time were being paid by companies which had an interest in the decisions of that committee. They used Mr. Kerlin, who also received a salary from Seaboard World Airlines—a beneficiary of part of about $100 mil-

lion a year paid by our government for hauling mail to
and from U.S. military bases overseas, according to newspaper reports.

Jerry Kluttz, former *Washington Post* staff writer,
once wrote he saw Kerlin come out of the closed-door session of a subcommittee that drafted a postal-rate-in-
crease bill. This brought a storm of accusations and
innuendoes because such practices are against congressional rules. Mr. Kerlin denied he had been in the room;
Mr. Kluttz countered that Kerlin had not denied it the
following Tuesday, and had simply stated that he wished
the article had not been written as it might lessen his influence. Mr. Kerlin also added, "I try to be helpful to
members of Congress. I guess I've written about 400 bills
and I expect to write about 400 more before I quit."

In our country lobbyists have their place. If a cause
isn't represented by a lobbyist it may be lost. Our government has subsidized almost anything and everything.
Billions for wars. Billions for old or new countries. Cash
for the soil bank program. Price guaranties for what was
grown. Even tax allowances for oil wells. But when it
came to money for personal, first class-mail for which
there were no lobbyists, it seemed to some as if the con-
sensus of our legislators was that non-lobbied mail could
go to hell.

The affinity of money and politics and vice versa is
comparable to the case of the chicken and the egg. Which
comes first? For instance, the top salary that could be
paid to a postmaster in our country was around $40,000.
The postmaster of New York City was overseeing the
work of the 49,000 employees who service the mail needs
of several million people. Drawing about the same salary
was another postmaster heading only about 85 employees
with a few hundred customers.

The difference? The second man was the postmaster
of the House of Representatives! To top it all, there was
a move afoot by this man's friends in Congress to raise

his salary closer to the salaries enjoyed by congressmen themselves. It seemed the closer you got to the power the more you were worth.

Many people have an aversion to any hanky-panky at all in the body that writes the laws of the land. But regardless of individual ideas on the subject, it remains a fact of life that our democratic processes are complicated and have their own peculiar ways that only a mellowed man can accept.

Another type of politics may be seen in the tactics employed by groups like the Direct Mail Advertising Association and the Associated Third-Class Mail Users. Harry J. Maginnis, president of the latter accused the newspapers of bombarding the public with complaints about the comparatively low rates of third-class mail because third-class mail competes with newspapers for the advertising dollar. He further claimed that the newspaper conspiracy against third-class mail advertising could only be described as a venal attempt to enrich the newspapers by destroying a competitor. Continuing, he claimed the newspapers thought it all right to plead their own cause before Congress but immoral for him to lobby for the 300,000 holders of third-class mailing permits on a matter which vitally affected their businesses.

Maginnis brought out what he called the "sacred cow" of the mails—the so-called red-tag handling of newspapers and news magazines whereby they got letter-class handling for the payment of newspaper rates. He figured at that time the *Wall Street Journal* was paying two cents per copy for an average weight of six ounces and if the proper postage were paid, its owners, the Dow Jones Co., would owe $280,000 more in postage every day, or $20 million more a year!

Though the postmaster may josh about "junk mail," he realizes it helps pay his salary. In fact, headquarters —in an effort at propriety—has instructed everyone not to use the term at all. It is offensive and improper to cer-

tain firms and people. It all depends on whose mail you
are talking about. One man's junk is another man's
fortune.

For years the unfairness of first-class mail subsidiz-
ing the other mail rates had been denounced, but the
situation remained about the same. The Congressional-
postal liaison consistently fixed it so a citizen was practically forced to accept all mail. If he notified the local
post office to put no third-class mail in his box, this would
necessarily include his license tags, tax forms, election
materials and church and civic notices.

The sponsors of periodic proposals to take the low
cost mail advantages away from big businesses knew all
the time their bills didn't have a chance of passage. They
were introduced for their propaganda value. Brother
Bean, our mail service moralist, when speaking against
postal pressure groups was wont to remark, "Live by the
sword—die by the sword!" Maybe that's the story of the
Post Office Department. Politicians caused it to rise, politicians caused it to fall!

The immortal Will Rogers also commented: "It's
awful hard to get people interested in corruption unless
they can get some of it." But then to show that he had not
lost faith in our American system, he added: "Times
have proven that you can't ruin this country with politics!" This is as applicable to the mails as to the country
in general.

14. Pornography or Art?

The Post Office, of necessity, has continually left its doors wide open for contemptuous laughter to flow forth. At the time when the public had been reading in the newspapers for months about the legal contest between the Department and a publisher named Ralph Ginsburg who sought to sell his publications through the mails, Ginsburg announced to the press that his archenemy had invited him to a party. He had received an invitation to see the postmaster general swear in the new postmaster of New York City.

Using the occasion to prick his adversaries, Ginsburg announced to reporters, "It's either a colossal blunder of a great practical joke, most likely a colossal blunder." The Post Office said it was neither. He got the invitation because he was "one of the large volume mailers in Manhattan."

For practically its entire lifetime, the post office has been involved in a fervent fight against whatever the current mores of society deemed to be undesirable. In 1872, the Young Men's Christian Association of New York formed a Commission for the Suppression of Vice. Heading it was an individual whose name came to be a household word and his reputation a legend in his own time.

Postal Americana would not be complete without mention of Anthony Comstock. He successfully beleaguered Congress to pass a law against obscenity—which

115

came to be called the Comstock Law—and the Post Office appointed him a special agent, without pay, to help enforce it. He was within his rights to confiscate—for the purpose of gathering evidence for the prosecutors—all sorts of sex-oriented items including "articles made of rubber for immoral purposes." This man spent forty years of his life crusading against the vices of his era.

Although today we hear a lot about the proliferation of pornographic material in the mails, it is doubtful that the ratio of objectionable matter to total quantity of mail is any greater now than it was during the era when Comstock was crusading. A hundred years ago the mail volume was only two or three percent of what it is today. And we have become somewhat acclimated to all sorts of obscenity in our midst. But being aware of the increased moral laxity and the upsurge in crime which many attribute to pornography, most postal employees have felt like a sewer pipe when they were forced to convey unordered filth.

Interestingly, what may be considered indecent by one person may be quite natural for another. Something obnoxious to one person is art to another. So what is obscenity? The judiciary has been quite cagey about this. For one person may go to court as quickly to defend his right to possess as another would to attempt to dispossess.

This lack of concurrence regarding pornography may be construed as an adjunct of our modern capitalistic-democratic concepts. How our government can and does work was evidenced by the rider sponsored by Rep. Glenn Cunningham and Rep. J. R. Waldie which was attached to the postage rate-salary increase bill passed in December of 1967. The rider stated that any householder could decide if material received in the mail was "erotically arousing or sexually provocative" to himself or anyone under 19 years of age in his residence.

If a patron filed a complaint on the prescribed form, the Post Office would have the responsibility to see that this household was excluded from this mailing list. The law applied to mail simply addressed to occupant or household as well as that specifically addressed to individuals. To its advocates this statute was seen to give the master of the house the same right to prevent unwelcome mail coming into his home as he would have to prevent an intruder. Those opposed argued that the senders have the right to communicate with anyone under the free speech amendment to the Constitution; if the recipient doesn't want the missive, he can discard it.

Immediately upon the passage of the law, which became effective in April 1968, steps were taken to challenge the rider. Organizations like the Direct Mail Advertising Association were quite interested. Due to the problems of enforcing the edict, it was felt by many that at least tacit support was given to the opposition by the Post Office Department. However in 1970, the courts upheld the law anyway.

To illustrate the complexity of complaints, many people protested that the form which the complainant completed—giving names and ages of household members —simply supplied the undesirable-mail peddlers with free lists of names, and let them know when the youngsters became nineteen years of age.

Therefore, on February 1, 1971, a subsequent law took effect which permitted people to file—at the post office from which they received their mail—a form which only averred they considered the material to be sexually provocative. The Postal Service was then required to see that the mailer deleted this patron's name from their list. Many people filled out the forms that banned undesirable mail to themselves, specifying that everything from frying pans to panty hose turned them on! By the latter part of 1971 about 410,000 Americans had asked the Postal Service to put their names on lists barring them from receiving such mail.

When in March 1966, the Supreme Court upheld an

obscenity by mail conviction of Ralph Ginsburg, it ruled
in effect that the advertisement of a product may be considered by the courts in deciding whether the product
itself is obscene. Most of the mailings about which postal
patrons complain are not legally obscene. Many of these
are ads for sex-aid devices, generally written with an
attempt to convey the impression of medical sanction.
Hard core pornography is considered to be pictures of
the sex act and sex perversions. Anything less than this
is simply frowned upon.

Congress passed a law in 1967 creating a commission to ponder pertinent questions and compile data on
smut. On January 2, 1968, President Johnson got around
to appointing the eighteen members to this Commission
on Obscenity and Pornography. An office was set up and
a staff hired for hearings, investigations and the prepa-
ration of the voluminous reports to be submitted by January 31, 1970. In keeping with the standards of the times,
this became another alphabet soup commission (COP).
Considering that the members were allowed over two
years in which to view pornography and seventy-five dollars a day each on commission business, they were expected to be able to come up with a pretty good report.

On August 11, 1970 the House Subcommittee on
Postal Operations listened to testimony regarding some
of the federally sponsored experiments which had been a
part of this $2 million program. The researchers had
been thorough. On occasions they employed an instrument called a plethysmograph which measured the increase in size of the penis while the subject viewed pornography. Another method involved analyzing urine for
acid phosphatase, an enzyme found in the prostatic fluid.
After listening to the testimony, Rep. H. R. Gross
(R-Iowa) summed up the feelings of the committeemen
by labeling the report "a tragic waste of the taxpayers
money."

Meanwhile, the average number of complaints about

obscene mail still run between 100,000 and 200,000 annually. In recent years the Inspection Service has investigated thousands of instances, effecting hundreds of arrests. Very little hard core pornography that originates in the United States is put into the postal stream nowadays, though. The operators do their own transportation to avoid prosecution under the mail statutes. But it is not unusual to have the mails saturated with stuff originating in foreign places, principally Scandinavia. The patrons read advertisements and send their orders directly to the foreign country.

Until January, 1971—when the Post Office was required to cease the practice—a court order was generally obtained against the sender of obscenity prohibiting his use of the U.S. mails. Then should a post office see mail with the offender's return address or name as sender, the mail could be stamped Unlawful and not delivered to the addressee. Similarly, if mail was observed being sent to the offender's address or person, it was stamped and returned to the sender.

Typically though, the department had always been lax in enforcing these "illegal orders;" and many postal clerks had a very liberal attitude in this respect. Coming across bare pulchritude inbound from the Scandinavian countries was considered by many to be one of the fringe benefits of certain postal jobs.

People openly display today what they would have hidden a couple of generations ago—from ankles to postal hobbies. An acquaintance proudly exhibits his collection of picture postcards postmarked at places with names centering on sex: Intercourse, Middlesex, Virginville, etc. He, in all sincerity, considers this a valid part of mail Americana. And whenever any pornography is detected in a post office, you may depend on some employees to announce to the rest, "Look, there's some obscene mail!"

15.　U.S.A. to U.S.A. & P.

International mail, once a rarity, may now be equated to domestic mail of yesteryear. In 1971 about 500 million pounds of international mail left this country— and it did not advertise local sales, politicians or the like.

The subject of international mail immediately brings up the matter of equitable payment of postage to the country performing the service. A world postage stamp, good in any country, has long been advocated but differences in currencies have been a serious drawback. However, the question of one country receiving an inequitable share of revenue from the sale of stamps for articles to be delivered in other countries has not seriously been raised under our present system. It surely would in a universal stamp system. Variable exchange rates could be a source of profiteering in postage, as has happened. Private businessmen are always looking for ways to bring money into their coffers and often they can move faster than governmental bureaucracies.

Quite likely a universal postage system will eventually be developed. Internationally uniform weights and measures is a step in this direction. But for the present, the best we can offer are International Reply Coupons. These were suggested by an Austrian, Ritter von Raimann and effected by the Universal Postal Union. They may be purchased at a post office in one country and redeemed in another for sufficient postage to send a letter back to the purchaser.

How a country desires to run the internal affairs of its postal administration is largely its own business. It can use its stamps as it sees fit. But even though it may elect to turn the operation of its internal postal services over to private business or a quasi-governmental agency, its participation in the intercourse of foreign mail is still governed by international law. Arrangements between nations regarding postal matters are handled and governed by the unique organization mentioned above.

In 1863, representatives from seventeen governments, offering infant international postal service, met in Paris at the suggestion of the U.S. postmaster general to formulate plans for an organization to facilitate the transmission of mail from one country to another. This was the beginning of the Universal Postal Union. Now a part of the United Nations, the U.P.U. represents the most sincere efforts the world has seen to promote common good through communications.

On the international level great dignity is given to mail. In the United States the general interpretation of "the sanctity of the seal" is the right to secretiveness in a letter, but a lot of foreign countries place more importance on the letters. They agree with St. Paul's statement in 2 Corinthians 10:10, ". . . . what we say by letter when absent, we do when present." When viewed in this light, a letter represents something very much alive and personal; thus it follows that appropriate dignity be given to the physical delivery of such mail.

It is reassuring that there exists today the same quality of service that Ralph Waldo Emerson referred to in his essay "On Civilization," where he said: "The power of a wafer to guard a letter as it flies over sea, over land, and comes to its address as if a battalion of artillery brought it, I look upon as a fine meter of civilization."

You often hear comparisons of postal service in the United States, Germany, England and other countries; but for the most part they are not comparable. The Brit-

ish post office operates over an area no larger than our
state of Oregon. Our country handles more than seven
times the amount of mail it does but we have only four
times as many employees as she. Does this mean that the
American postal employee is more productive than the
British? In fact, the United States has fewer employees
in relation to mail handled than Germany, Italy, France,
Belgium, Japan, Holland or Switzerland.

The range of duties must be taken into account also.
The German and English mails are operated as parts of
an all-encompassing communications system. Post offices
in Britain provide banking facilities, lend money, rent
computer services, sell government securities and license
home radios and televisions. They even sell chances in a
weekly lottery run by the government!

The German system, called the Bundespost, makes a
profit of over $40 million each year and the British sys-
tem makes a profit of over $20 million. The U.S. Post Of-
fice lost a billion dollars in 1971; but then the United
States handles nearly as much mail in a month as do
Britain or Germany in a year. The postal system of the
little Netherlands turned in a big profit of $45 million in
a recent year. But their telegraph and telephone service
is included, and the mail end of the operation actually
lost over $13 million. These countries have less of the so-
called junk mail than the United States and their smaller
size contributes to their profitable operations.

The German postal system makes money on its telephone business and letter delivery, but loses heavily on
parcels, paper and telegram distribution. If our Postal
Service had the profits from the U.S. telephone and telegram businesses, couldn't it pour the red ink down the
drain!

Germany uses a pneumatic tube system between airports and post offices, and between various offices. Paradoxically, the United States has for the most part aban-
doned the pneumatic tube system that was in effect,

primarily in New York City. On the other hand Paris has effectively used an underground network for special delivery mail for a hundred years. Letters can reach any part of Paris within an hour via the 250 miles of tubes which connect the post offices. At the terminals, motorcycle mailmen are waiting to rush the letters to their destinations. They might, however, arrive a little crumpled, oily or slightly soiled, as the suction tubes are all built into the sewer mains!

Russia has headaches from her vastness. The lack of population density is a very real factor in her postal operations. While England has 852 persons per square mile and the United States only 49; Russia has just 24. The duties of the Russian post offices are about as diversified as ours, though. While we do such things as register aliens, they accept payments from telephone and TV subscribers and act as the agent for state banks.

In Russia the per capita mail count is still only about a hundred pieces per year—compared to more than four hundred in the United States—although the Ministry of Postal and Electrical Communications reports that their mail volume has about doubled in the past five years. Their 88,000 offices handle about 40 billion pieces of mail a year, whereas our 32,000 offices handle more than 87 billion pieces. Peculiarly, most of the Russian mail is newspapers and magazines. Their letter mail is only one-fourth that of newspapers and magazines. In the United States that percentage is reversed.

This large volume of Soviet publications is attributable to the government's concerted efforts to educate the masses. The mails handle eighty-seven percent of the circulation of all the newspapers and magazines. Electronic devices reproduce major newspapers in the larger post offices, far away from the point of transmission, only minutes after publication.

We hear little about mail service in countries where service is not up to ours; but in many parts of the world, mail service is not much to write home about. In Mexico, a letter often takes several weeks for delivery. This is accepted and taken for granted. Mañana! In Chile a plate of escudos must be kept near the front door. The mailman is tipped every time he brings a letter.

Though that of the United States has been the most acute, every country has experienced a mail increase related to its population explosion. All major countries have been forced to devise a coding system to facilitate mail handling. The basic difference is in their names: *leitzahl* sounds as Teutonic as zip does American.

Although geographical customs affect mail services, the services all are kindred. Great Britain had just decided to turn its postal system and related activities into a corporation when Postmaster General Lawrence O'Brien proposed that we do likewise. Many of the British utilities—telephone, telegraph and post—were joined in a complex run by the government. The British encountered some major problems in the changeover. The U.S. commission studied those developments thoroughly, but one could not assume that things would work in this country as they did over there.

To illustrate the differences, the other day a newly arrived Britisher approached the post office at the Dulles International airport where I work and asked to convert his pounds to dollars and deposit most of the currency. I explained that most post offices in this country performed neither of these services. And after being subsequently informed that we also did not handle telegrams or telephone calls, he looked at me incredulously. Then his gaze fixed on a Wanted poster on the wall. Turning to me aghast, he said, "Inadequate as your post office already is, you're wanting desperate looking characters like that to work in it?"

A most unusual example of the services of the English post is that they permit live people to be mailed. After a drinking bout in a pub, it's an easy way to send an inebriated friend to his home—though rather costly, weight-wise.

Today, the increased impetus of internationalism puts great pressure on all to do away with such individualism. Through improved communications, places on the opposite sides of the globe are closer today than places a hundred miles apart were at the beginning of this century. Now there is hardly a place in the world that doesn't have some daily mail communications with the farthest reaches of the world.

We all live at a faster pace than before. Until the advent of instantaneous transmission of messages, the main notification of death and other important events was the letter. Now it's done by telephone, telegraph, cable, radio or even television. But the post still offers an inexpensive and private means to convey messages, and for this reason will be with us for a long time. It is nice to know that no place in the world is any farther away than the nearest mailbox.

Even though U.S. postal regulations specify that outgoing foreign mail must have the address in English, many people insist upon using terminology that is familiar to them. As old postal clerks continue to use the unofficial term *nixie*, so the public continues to use the older names of the foreign countries. It is common knowledge that Iran was formerly Persia and Abyssinia is now Ethiopia; but Soumi being Finland and Shqipni, Albania are horses of another color. You'll never see these names programmed into a computerized letter-sorting machine.

Some letter writers with a penchant for practical jokes address mail to "the only place in the North and South American continents where the sun rises in the Pacific and sets in the Atlantic Ocean." A look at the map showed that the writer could only be referring to Panama; a bend in the isthmus causes the singular situation.

That letter was delivered; but the public is well advised not to make puzzles of addresses.

Certain places mean so much to individuals they can't understand why it would need a full address. To them Pearl Harbor, Bastogne or their own personal Waterloo is sufficient. Articles having unclear addresses are decoded, if possible, in key post offices throughout the nation designated as exchange offices. These are located at major international terminals: Miami, New Orleans, Houston, New York, Chicago, Washington, etc. All outgoing international mail is funneled into these concentration points where it is prepared and dispatched. The exchange offices also receive and work international mail as it reaches this country.

In the days when much of our foreign mail was not in clear English, any clerk in the exchange office with knowledge of a particular foreign language or country was assigned to work mail to and from that country. Many of these clerks were first-generation Americans. As the article passed through the hands of one of these experts, he would pencil the address on properly, if it was not readily discernible.

Not blessed with an inherited factual information, I was at a disadvantage when assigned to work foreign mail. I felt compelled to assimilate all I could, correlate it in some semblance of order and preserve it. I began making notes of the "hards" I encountered as a way to gain proficiency at the job. As my hip-pocket brain became voluminous, I had to begin grouping the information.

I claim no laurels for this lexicographic work. But I ended up with a quick reference that I could use successfully. After compiling a list of several hundred abbreviations, idioms and foreign spellings: A.O.E., Africa Occidential Espagna (Spanish East Africa), Ingleterra (England), Allemagne (Germany), Escocia (Scotland), Suecia (Sweden), Suiza (Switzerland), etc., I had a friend review the papers. He concluded his appraisal by asking if I knew that the word *idiom* came from the same root as *idiot*. So my efforts were christened *Bowyer's Idiot Book.*

All the peoples of the world tend to retain their geographical personalities. Those from New South Wales and the Irish Free State continue to assert their prerogative of writing simply N.S.W. and I.F.S., and they are respected for it. However, I wonder how they will fare in the future with modern technology.

We in the United States are prone to consider our ways and our nomenclature pretty unique; but the realm of international mail puts things into perspective. One becomes aware that U.S.A. could just as well stand for Union of South Africa as it does for United States of America, even when the address reads Virginia, U.S.A.

I thought I knew all the abbreviations until one day I received a letter addressed to U.S.A. & P. Upon investigation, I was told that since Hawaii had been admitted into the Union and was not in America, technically our country was now the United States of America and Polynesia!

Our nation will soon be celebrating its bicentennial, but the world continues to regard our country as young. Is it because we are part of what was originally called the New World? Actually, there are only twenty nations in the world older than the United States: China, Ethiopia, Japan, Denmark, Bhutan, Sweden, France, San Marino, Russia, England, Portugal, Andorra, Thailand, Spain, Switzerland, Monaco, Netherlands, Liechtenstein, Afghanistan and Nepal. Since 1932 nearly a hundred new countries have been created. But old or new, the single thing that can be depended upon to connect them all is international mail.

16. The Horse Goes in the Wrong Direction

The psyche of the Post Office, that monumental organization that has everything from a few mules to a $10 billion budget, is grounded to a great degree on its insignia. The horse seal which was in use prior to 1971, had been looked upon as outliving its usefulness.

During the period of vehement public criticism and the days of agonizing self-appraisal by the Post Office Department prior to its conversion to Postal Service, the old horse was construed to signify antiquation. However, many of the administrators reasoned that the department was so hard-pressed for a favorable image that it shouldn't knock the nostalgic gift horse. But, whenever you approached a uniformed postal employee and remarked about the fetching appearance of his horseman insignia, he was apt to point to the rider and retort: "Yeah, and that's a jackass!" He had a south-end view which was emblematic of the general snafu.

Compounding and confounding things, horses were going in all directions. It depended on whose insignia you looked at. Finally, some straight-thinkers came into the grandiose departmental headquarters building on Pennsylvania Avenue. They noticed their predecessors had left a beautiful mosaic, incorporating the compass points, laid in the marble floor. But the directions were wrong! That figured. And they knew the horse—the traditional symbol of misdirection—had to go too! The new regime was not willing to let its structures be known as stables and did not want to be known as mule skinners. They pushed Old Dobbin out the door with the department.

Aristotle in his wisdom could have been anticipating the rise and fall of our Post Office when he said: ". . . it is the nature of the products to be better than the activities." The timeless adage *Errare Humanum* ("To err is human") is also applicable. This is not to condone the actions of groups or individuals, but rather to state that we must accept philosophically the shortcomings that are inherent in as vast an undertaking as our Postal Service. The mails are worked by people and as such are subject to errors.

The rule books governing every official action and many off-the-clock activities of postal employees once weighed forty odd pounds. Each page was intended to bring about necessary regimentation and control of the work force and standardization of procedures, but the more rules we had the more confusion there was. In the old days, I had a supervisor who consistently judged his men by the number of error notices sent to him. Then every package of letters had the name of the clerk who prepared it on the facing slip with which it was tied, so responsibility for errors could be placed. It's one of the little things that mean so much but aren't done anymore.

Back then a man was expected to make a limited number of mistakes. But, according to the standards of the times, a man worth his salt wasn't likely to make the same error twice. In other words, a mistake was a sign of learning. Too often today a mistake is something that, gotten away with once, can be gotten away with again.

I believe any corporate entity can be likened to and described as having attributes of an individual. Psychiatry defines masochism as a perversion that causes a person to derive pleasure from punishment. I think the Post

Office has indulged in pathological masochism. It has loved to take a beating. On all sides the usual retort has been: "Well, what else can you expect from the Post Office?" Paradoxically, small segments of the postal creature could be observed to exude excessive narcissism. A happy medium had to be sought by the organization. Counseling and self-analysis were needed.

Contributing adversely to the confused postal personality was the habit of many newspaper makeup men of assigning articles about the Post Office to a section next to the comics. They always figured it laugh material! And the Post Office has been a laugh for all ages. An adolescent asks, "What two words have more letters than any other?" and answers "Ha Ha! The Post Office." As he ages, the words are equated to a kissing game. By the time he becomes an adult, he automatically grins when he utters the words.

Some anecdotes from the department files are funny. I remember when a new postal-truck driver in the District of Columbia was told to: "Take the New York mail;" and he did—to New York! First, though, he went home and picked up a relative for companionship on the long drive. He had to borrow some money to buy gas with, got lost on the way and was accosted by the highway patrol when he ran out of gas. He almost made it though; for after his extraordinarily long day's work, he was stalled only a few blocks from the main post office in New York City. We were a long time living that incident down, because it got into the newspapers. Unfortunately, nationwide—and next to the comic pages again!

Another postal truck driver confided to me that when he was new on the job he became confused and had to enquire of a pedestrian where the post office was. The first man he asked didn't know. The second man was so flustered he had difficulty giving coherent instructions.

How would you feel if a post office truck should stop you, inquiring where the post office was?

The ever-present critics keep fanning the sparks so the fire of postal foolery never dies. Former postmasters general go all over the country making after-dinner speeches ridiculing the Post Office. Larry O'Brien liked to say that the department reminded him of the old definition of an elephant: "A mouse built to government specifications." J. Edward Day, after he left the job, wrote what could be called a joke book about it. And in 1970 while postmen were wildcat striking for a wage increase, comedian Groucho Marx caustically said he had the perfect solution: "We give them their raise, but we mail it to them!"

Possibly one of the greatest disservices to the Post Office was when someone coined the phrase *junk mail*. Have you ever noticed that letter-drop boxes have been placed on sidewalks in close proximity to public trash receptacles? Or is it the other way around? Anyway, a psychiatrist or just plain student of human behavior would tell you that there is a connection between the two.

Possibly the accumulation of these little things broke down the morale and efficiency of the department as much as favoritism, which gets credit from those wise to its inner workings. Also playing a part was flim-flam like the savings bond campaigns when officials would say privately to their subordinates: "You've been wanting me to do something for you: so if you just subscribe to this bond plan, I'll go along." To make a good showing for themselves, supervisors were known to tell their employees to subscribe and later cancel the subscription. That way everybody would be happy.

Then, once a year there was the Combined Federal Campaign: the beseeching of government employees to give part of their salaries to organized charity. Some units consistently made a superior record on paper by having their employees sign a contribution pledge with the understanding that they could renege on the payment. After the campaign was over, the heat was off.

The Post Office too often belittled itself by its own actions. Maybe this is one of the reasons why, when you question a child about what he wants to be when he grows up, he mentions doctor, lawyer, fireman or policeman, but seldom postman. Remember the fable about the charlatan who sold the emperor a new suit with the admonition that the fabric would appear invisible to those who were stupid? Everyone enjoyed the parade until *les enfants* said: "Look—naked!"

When the veneer was stripped from the postal personality of the past you got some mighty frank statements. Some employees said they did not want to be equated with poverty—they said it was time the government stopped placing people in the Post Office simply to help out the anti-poverty program, and should instead build a hard-hitting crew who knew what had to be done and had the ability and desire to do it.

But the lack of ability and desire did not all come with anti-poverty activities. I once worked with a fellow who either couldn't or wouldn't take his case exams, the means of testing a clerk's knowledge of mail distribution requirements. He ended up being given an office job with no distribution-knowledge requirements—a job which should have gone to someone who had earned it. He was assigned because he wasn't qualified to do anything else; and he had the necessary pull to get the job. Later through friendship with the proper people, he was given a high-ranking job telling other people how to pass the same examinations he himself wouldn't or couldn't take!

One of the greatest drawbacks to a postal career had been the lack of opportunity for promotion. The Kappel Commission figured that less than one in ten employees had any hope of being elevated above the grade in which he began. There were a total of 750,000 postal employees and only 70,000 supervisory, postmaster and technical positions. A man hired as a clerk or carrier would probably retire as a clerk or carrier. He was in the Post Office, that notorious bawdy house of political plunder where the favored got what there was to be gotten.

The entrance pay for a postal worker was usually higher than an unskilled worker could get elsewhere. Initially the employee was glad to get the high starting wage rate, but several years later he felt he had been sucked into a dead-end job. Then around middle age he would just idle his motor and develop a philosophical outlook, becoming complacent with his niche in society and his job security.

His security was getting broader and his status more refined all the time.

A few years previously, if the boss considered that a clerk had the time, he could put a broom in his hands and tell him to sweep the floor. In fact junior clerks did most of this duty in spare moments. Now with unions and job descriptions, clerks can not be required to do this.

Though many postal employees would never consider themselves subservient to anyone, some of their patrons look upon everyone on the federal payroll as public servants in the most complete sense of the word. One day an ultrafastidious young lady came to the window, pushed a letter towards the clerk and ordered a six-cent stamp. The clerk thereupon pushed the stamp, gum up as required, towards the customer. She countered, "Am I supposed to stick it on myself?" The clerk retorted, "It would get more results if you stuck it on the letter."

During the several years immediately prior to the dissolution of the department, one could rarely pick up a newspaper which didn't have an article in it criticizing the Post Office. For the most part it was constructive. It seemed that a gargantuan monstrosity had been created and its warped tentacles could not be controlled.

There was a built-in inefficiency factor. Oklahoma congressman Tom Steed summed up PMG O'Brien's testimony by saying: "As manager of the Post Office Department, you have no control of these employees, virtually no control of the physical facilities you are forced to use, and only limited control at best over the transportation facilities."

It is a practice in each post office that one of the junior employees runs up the U.S. flag at the start of the business each morning. Perhaps symbolic of the department's straits, at this time in postal history, when the banner got displayed upside-down—the universal signal of distress—some offices were said never to right it.

Between the act of February 20, 1792, making detailed provisions for an official Post Office Department and its demise, the organization was racked with ineptitude in many areas and ways. At its birth it had congenital defects, and the ill genes of regulations, procedures, customs, patronage and nepotism shackled each succeeding generation. It was not surprising that the flood of fallibility finally inundated everyone and brought about the death of the department.

Few mourned.

17. An Eagle to Surmount the Problems

On August 12, 1970, as President Nixon signed into law the act which created the new Postal Service, Postmaster General Blount unveiled the new seal. It had become official two days previous when filed with the secretary of state. Replacing the old horse-and-rider seal, referred to variously as a nag, jackass, donkey, mule, etc., was what the PMG hailed as the new "stylicized (sic) Federal Eagle." But military veterans present, remembering the emblem issued to mustered-out personnel at the end of World War II, immediately piped up: "Look, there's our old Ruptured Duck!"

Some say the postal seal should be again changed. If the Treasury Department can do it right, so can the Postal Service. In 1968 that department quietly adopted a new seal; the most significant change was in its 200-year-old wording. In lieu of Seal of the Treasury of North America they substituted: The Department of the Treasury. Unlike the Post Office which eliminated the word *department*, the Treasury put it in. The wording ". . . of North America" was the vestige of our founding fathers' hope that Canada would join the states. A few people who had noticed the wording thought of the U.S. taxpayer's money being squandered all over the world and suggested a more appropriate change: Seal of the Treasury of the Whole Damned World!

Now since the Post Office is also supposed to have a more appropriate look, some would like to see its seal given more ecumenical significance. They would put the horses, mules, eagles and ducks back in the barnyard and present a winged earth centered in a three-way clasp of brown, white and yellow hands signifying the communication of modern mankind.

Be its symbol duck, donkey or eagle, the U.S. Postal Service is the most human institution operated by our government: the means by which the federalcy maintains a continuing contact with each of its citizens. The employees are covered by what the general public considers very good benefits from recruitment to retirement. Firstly, they can transfer from one office to another with relative ease until they find a niche they fit comfortably. Lastly, whenever the job gets boring, they can always read somebody's postcards—even though the practice is forbidden.

With all the benefits, the postal employee should have been happy in his job, but in actuality the opposite was true. The satisfied postmaster of the small town became a minority, and the majority of employees were discontent to the point where their efficiency was impaired and the discontentment generated more of the same. From the end of World War II until the postal revolution of '71, morale was low.

Though the employees were well equipped to vocalize their complaints through grievance procedures, set up by the unions, they were constantly clamoring for management to stamp out inequities, real or imaginary. Those who worked the night shift said they deserved more than their ten percent additional pay between the hours of 6 P.M. and 6 A.M.—for only policemen, prostitutes and postal clerks have to work such hours. Their job could be equated to no other and they made the most of the disparity.

Management, like the other bureaucracies of our government, too often ran hot and cold. In one instance you could question something and get no answer to your query; another time their reply would tell you how to build a watch. Sometimes when a written memo would do, they'd send a man out to describe the situation. I guess they figured it's hard to describe something going around in circles without waving one's hands. To top it all off, the ratio of men to mail, or vice versa, was often a yoyo pattern; there was either too much mail and too few men, or too many men and not enough mail.

The employees did not presume to tell all the postal managers how to run their business. Some administrators wished to exercise their prerogative to run (or ruin) their own show and realized the operation was like a bicycle—it had to be peddled or it would fall down. Unfortunately, many of the so-called managers didn't care which direction the vehicle was going as long as it didn't fall over while they were riding it. After all, why worry: didn't a lot of postal administrators have the power to do nothing?

Whether the Post Office should be run as a service subsidized by the government or an organization that pays its own way has never been resolved; and it is doubtful if it ever will be. The problem has existed from the early days of our nation. Opponents to self-sufficiency say it would make as much sense to put the highway program on a self-supporting basis as it would the postal program. Considering this continuing indetermination, it was charged that our Post Office, like its so-called stylicized eagle, resembled some creature from ancient mythology, half beast and half bird—neither fish nor fowl.

Though times and methods change, the basic problem of getting a letter from one person at one place to another person at another place remains the same. In the early part of this century, it was the practice for men on a large workroom floor to wear roller skates to speed mail from one end of the room to another. It was the best way that had been devised at that time; now it is considered amusing. As times change, so do people. If it had been determined in the sixties that roller skates were still best, I doubt if the mail clerks could have been gotten to wear them. The old adage "If you can't rise in your profession, raise the profession" had become outmoded, out of place and unused.

Then again, some things were imposed with the simple exhortation that it was the "modern" thing to do. When the cost control system was initiated, it seemed as if a little education had proven to be worse than none at all. Once, the stiffly starched methods-and-standards-men walked in and gave my boss some new instructions. They also gave him a pair of dice and a little box to keep them in. He was to select a dozen pigeon-hole cases into which letters are distributed and number them from one to twelve. Each day he was to throw the dice and the number coming up would be the number of the case that the count would be taken on that day.

Seriously, I think this was the first time Joe Shanks ever had a pair of dice in his hands. He was from the old school and very narrow minded when it came to things like alcohol, women and games of chance. He could only roll "snake eyes." I showed him how to buck them and then he could only roll "box cars." He claimed the dice were loaded. I made no claims, the department boys were doing all that for me.

Once when I was discussing the more profound aspects of his job with one of the cost-control fellows, he smilingly told me that he overheard his wife, in answer to a neighbor inquiring what he did, reply "Well, if a woman did it, it would be called nagging."

Though the subjects of their scrutiny came to criticize them as they criticized us, I have to admit that someone who is totally unfamiliar with a business may have an insight into it that escapes those working with it for years; and I assume this is the reasoning behind it all. Why else would highly paid men be brought in to do things that confounded us so much? Although realizing that some of them were working just so headquarters could say they were providing modern management techniques, I am just naive enough to believe that they couldn't be a hundred percent "goof balls." But I think the method in their madness was often misguided.

How else could you rationalize that a methods analyst could justify any given set of facts, and back it up with supporting figures. Someday, one of them will have the letter carriers walking sideways because he has proven that it (1) would cost the government less through narrower sidewalks, (2) the carriers would already be facing the letter boxes they were to serve and (3) it would be safer because a greater area of their feet would be on the ground.

That makes as much sense as the system we had for arriving at certain figures concerning international mails. The system, bought lock, stock and barrel by the department, was full of holes. For example, on the printed sheets (official POD forms) devised by the men who prepared the system were blanks designated for the tabulation of certified mail. There wasn't any. International mail has no such classification.

What does all this prove? According to official postal records, efficiency increased every year. This, too, was a part of the efficiency expert's record keeping. Common sense should dictate that if an operation is adjudged to be at seventy percent maximum efficiency, after increasing it five percent more than seven times you've proven your first figures wrong.

And errors were not restricted to accounting and work efficiency. They were represented in the operational fields as well. For instance, anyone who has done any flying knows how baggage is tagged to show where it is to be off-loaded. The tag will show the official airlines designation code of that city: JFK for Kennedy airport, LGA for La Guardia, SFO for San Francisco, etc. The code DIA was assigned to Dulles International airport.

Fine, until one realizes there is a hush-hush government agency in Washington known as the Defense Intelligence Agency (DIA).

This agency gets communications from certain overseas military units, which may be sent in a U.S. mail service rotary lock pouch. This pouch has a special brass lock with a window in it which shows, like the odometer on your car, a progressively higher number every time the lock is opened. The lock number plus the window number constitute the number of that registered dispatch. This is the prescribed way to send more important registered mail from one point to another.

One particular time, the military postal unit preparing the dispatch did not fully print out the name of the intended addressee: Defense Intelligency Agency, on the pouch label, but simply abbreviated DIA, Wash., D.C. My registry clerk quite naturally thought it was mail for our postal facility (DIA), opened the pouch and found nothing but an envelope in it. It also read DIA. He opened it but was unable to decipher the writing, which was in the Defense Department's own brand of hieroglyphics. As I came upon the scene, he had written boldly across the face of the paper, "We don't understand this at DIA."

This mistake can not be attributed to John Foster Dulles, from whom the airport gets its name. You'd be surprised at the number of grown people who don't know or remember who John Foster Dulles was and spell the word *Dullas*. This similarity has sent a lot of mail to the wrong airport, half-way across the nation. No misspelling is necessary to confuse Dulles with Dallas, the similarity in sound is enough.

Another agency in Washington doing classified work is the Defense Communications Agency. Yes, that's right. The use of their initials caused similar situations at National Airport, also coded DCA. How many other such situations have existed throughout the country?

All units dispatching mail have to be very careful. A wrong code can make a world of difference, particularly regarding mail for connecting flights. To this end, I tried for years to get the code for Dulles changed. It was always somebody else's jurisdiction. After nearly six years of snafu, it was changed to IAD effective May 23, 1968. Now there's only a remote possibility of misdirecting mail; the most similar destination code is LAD for far-off Luanda, Angola, Africa.

The Post Office was one of the few major governmental institutions that had not substantially contributed to the world of technology. To name a few, Public Health, Interior, Space, Agriculture—even the military, have contributed to the improvement of mankind. For the most part, the Post Office simply floated with the tide. The zip code was probably its greatest claim to fame; but even this was brought about primarily by the technology of the customers. Most of what came into the mailstream was bulk material prepared by the mailers. Actually, forty percent of the mail consisted of commercial transactions (bills, etc.), twenty-six percent advertising, eleven percent newspapers and magazines and only twenty-two percent personal correspondence.

The bulk mailers modernized their operations with the use of automatic data processing (ADP) equipment. It was just one step further for them to pre-sort their mail before depositing it in a post office. The General Accounting Office of the federal government had used individually assigned numbers to identify post offices many years before the Post Office Department authorized any numerical code to work mail with. The celebrated zip code just sort of evolved. Officially, it was initiated in 1963, as the result of an idea proposed by Washington, D.C. postal manager, Bentley Hahn.

I had sent in an employee suggestion that the de-

partment adopt codes for all offices before zip was
adopted. My system was to utilize combinations of the
digits one through nine in combination with all twenty-
six letters of the alphabet, making a three symbol code.
Remember how much easier it was to remember a phone
number that began with two letters?

Prior to zip code, each of the approximately 35,000
offices, in essence, exchanged mail with all the others. By
using the code, mail was routed through only 552 sectional centers, designated by the first three digits of the
zip code. Bulk mailers could arrange their correspond-
ent's addresses in zip-code sequence and use Automatic
Data Processing machines to pre-sort their mail and sack
it by zip number. It could be dispatched directly to the
proper office without being opened or worked until it
got to its destination.

Under our old system addresses had to be read by
as many as ten employees before the mail was finally
delivered, each reading consuming valuable time and add-
ing another chance of human error. With zip, the clerks
needed only sort by the numbers which eliminated much
memorization of routing schemes and provided better
service at less cost to the public.

The zip code has had some completely unplanned
uses. A salesman sent to work in an area could be preceded by a direct mailing to the customers or prospects
selected by three key digits in their zip code. A store,
plant or sales office could determine where it would be
most advantageous to locate a facility by determining
from the zip codes where the bulk of their customers
lived. A nursery owner could combine zip code data with
Department of Agriculture data on the frost line, to
determine when to mail to certain areas.

The number of mail-carrying trains declined from
over ten thousand in 1930 to only a handful by the time
of the postal reorganization. During this period, mail
volume increased from 27 billion to more than 87 billion

pieces per year. Most of the old ways of transportation had gone with the wind. To fly mail, it had to be worked at concentration points; the zip code was a simple way to direct it to these places.

Everyone knows the population of our country continues to rise, but most don't realize that our mail volume has always risen even faster. In 1946 we had 141 million people in the United States. In 1971 we had over 204 million—an increase of forty percent. During this same period, mail volume doubled. Until the 1960's, any rise in mail volume was followed by a like rise in the authorized personnel complement of an office. If that principle had continued, eventually every man, woman and child in the United States would have been in the Postal Service.

So it was seen that a horse—not even a post pony— could wade through the mountain of mail; it would take an eagle to surmount it.

18.   No New Ideas

Almost every American has analyzed the ills of his post office. Considering that, at the time of the Kappel Commission investigation in 1968, the department had to hire and train three workers to end up with one permanent employee and one-third of its employees had less than three years of service, one has to admit that, neurotic or not, the ills of the institution were not psychosomatic.

Contributing to this condition was the large number of the jobs that had to do with handling complaints; one wonders how a pleasing personality was maintained at all. Though many people didn't bother to register them formally, the management was receiving more than 300,-000 complaints annually. Striving to cut down on these criticisms, each new president recommended that postal rates be increased.

This was never the right answer for the Post Office Department. Three built-in factors were the basis of many shortcomings. Firstly, it could not control its workload (and still can't). The public determines this. Secondly, it had no control over its finances. Revenues went to the U.S. Treasury; and the department had to apply to the Bureau of the Budget and depend on Congress to appropriate operating funds. Thirdly, it could not control the price it charged for its services. Postal rates were set by Congress.

The criticisms of postal operations provided daily

reading in the nation's newspapers. On February 27, 1967 Postmaster General Lawrence O'Brien told the House Appropriations Committee: "Gentlemen, though I dislike opening my testimony on a discouraging note, I would fail in my responsibility towards the American people if I did not say, frankly, that at present your Post Office Department is in a race with catastrophe. And it is a race that we could well lose, though it is certainly in our power not to lose it."

For three weeks during the Christmas rush of 1966 the main Chicago post office did not function. Trains and trucks loaded with mail tied up traffic at all entrances. Total paralysis set in. This situation was corrected only by flying mail away from Chicago to be sorted. Allegedly the stoppage was brought about by a massive employee slowdown coupled with general mismanagement.

Urging that something constructive be done about our mail service before unthinkable chaos should occur, in March of 1967 Senator Daniel Brewster of Maryland referred to this debacle: ". . . in Chicago and, to a lesser degree, elsewhere in this country, we had a foretaste of what can happen if we do not act intelligently and courageously. We saw a total collapse of the mail service—millions of pounds of mail piled up without sufficient men and machines to work it, first-class letters delayed as long as three weeks before delivery—shameful suggestions that the only way to get rid of the mail was to burn it."

The tempo of public criticism of the postal establishment increased. Then on April 3, 1967, the postmaster general shocked the public by suggesting in a speech to the Magazine Publishers Association and the American Society of Magazine Editors that the Post Office Department be done away with. He proposed instead that the mails be handled by a nonprofit corporation which could provide such services as might be authorized by Congress. It should be operated by a board of directors appointed

by the president and confirmed by Congress, and man-
aged by a professional executive appointed by the board,
who would no longer be a member of the president's cabinet. Mr. O'Brien pointed out that not only mail volume
but the quagmire of legislation and custom that envel-
oped the system in the century and a half since its birth,
prompted his proposal.

Naturally this created quite a stir throughout the
United States. A member of the cabinet was suggesting
that his job be abolished! One of the highest presidential
appointees was stating to the world that one of the departments of the United States government was not
workable. This dramatically emphasized to the American
public that the mail service wasn't what it used to be.

The president immediately appointed a blue-ribbon
committee to study the proposal for a year and then
report to him. So the President's Commission on Postal
Organization, known as the Kappel Commission, set up
shop in Washington, D.C. After spending a million dollars, the jury reported back to the president in April of
1968 as expected. Verdict? Guilty on all counts! Recommendation? Death!

Before the sentence of the 212-page Kappel Commission indictment could be imposed, stamps of approval
were necessary from both houses of Congress. Democratic
processes dictated that all defenses be heard and all consequences considered. Many opposed the capital penalty
and favored rejuvenation within the framework of the
old structure. And there were opportunists looking for a
situation they might take advantage of. What course
should history take?

Many of those unwilling to go along with euthanasia
for the aged department changed sides in 1970, when at
midnight on March 17th, a wildcat pay-raise strike
started in New York City and in the succeeding three
days spread to fourteen states and included nearly 210,-
000 of the nation's postal workers. The postmen had

made their point. The mailman was discovered when he wasn't there!

It was a national emergency. The president of the United States ordered the Armed Forces into the post offices to work the mail. When television showed the soldiers sorting mail while postmen picketed outside, many citizens had new thoughts.

Although the idea that mail services need not be operated by the government was aired periodically, generally after announcements of the operating deficits of the department, few had ever thought seriously of there not being a federal postman to bring mail. Now they realized that the United States could very well get out of the mail-carrying business. Mr. Justice Holmes' legal opinion was cited: "The United States may give up the Post Office when it sees fit."

O'Brien's suggestion of a semi-governmentally operated post was anything but new. When this country was still a part of the British Empire, a private postal system was operated in thirty cities by William Goddard, a Baltimore publisher. But the concept was controversial even then. In 1843 PMG Charles A. Wickliffe suggested private operation in his annual report. During McKinley's administration, a report by the Post Office Committee of the House ridiculed the idea that postal service had to be offered by the government. The report maintained that the system could be operated at the same rates by private industry and return a profit every year. In 1932, PMG Walter F. Brown told Congress that the mails could be more efficiently handled as a private business. And most recently, after fourteen months of study, the Hoover Commission had come up with the same findings in 1948 that the Kappel Commission was destined to restate.

As had Britain's postologist Sir Rowland Hill, knowingly or unknowingly, appropriated an idea enunciated two hundred years before when he "invented" postage stamps, so America's orator of the hour, the renowned Mr. O'Brien, wearing the hat of postmaster general, dipped into the past and plucked out a concept for the future. As it turned out, he had made a good speech; it made sense. Those wise to the ways of men observed, "It will probably make sense again, years from now, when someone else adopts O'Brien's idea."

President Johnson's concurrence with his postmaster general added credence to any proposal for revision. Few would deny that major changes were necessary; but those administering postal business were politically oriented and their statements were always viewed in a political context. Larry O'Brien's predecessor J. Edward Day took issue with the proposal and opposed the corporation plan. Likewise, Congressman Thaddeus Dulski, chairman of the House Post Office and Civil Service Committee, questioned the wisdom of the plan which would at least theoretically, take politics out of the postal establishment and eliminate the influence of Congress.

O'Brien resigned to manage Hubert Humphrey's unsuccessful bid for the presidency and was replaced with W. Marvin Watson, who appointed a group of his own men to study the study that had been studied. Then after a tenure of only eight months, Watson went out with the Johnson administration.

The plan voiced by the Democratic team of Johnson and O'Brien soon was picked up by the Republicans and used as a campaign issue. They promised action, which explains the adamant insistence on change by Nixon and Blount.

When the Kappel Commission report was only one-week old, Congressman Dulski eloquently summed up the feeling of many people: ". . . the presentation of a plan of such grave consequences by our top postal authority is the final evidence—if more evidence is needed —of the crisis in postal affairs that hangs like a sword of Damocles over the heads of 200 million Americans.

The postmaster general obviously shares the view of many qualified observers that the postal service can no longer go creaking along under a space age mandate hitched to a horse and buggy motive power—that the whole mammoth patchwork of postal activities must soon collapse like the legendary one-horse shay without deep and incisive surgery."

The public was ready to take up the knife itself, much to the dismay of postal employees. They, of course, were concerned about what might happen to their pay and benefits—matters regulated by Congress. The Lloyd-LaFollette Act of 1912 guaranteed them the right to petition their representatives in Congress. What would happen to this right?

Union opponents assumed the postal unions would oppose anything that would detract from their power, determined ultimately by two main factors. The first is the number of employees belonging and the second is the innate need for the unions. Many people figured there would be less need of unions if the malignant situation were bettered.

In any discussion of removing the mails from the direct control of the representative government, the fallacious argument that the new management could increase postal rates without the advice and consent of anyone always cropped up. The other universal topic was patronage. The Kappel Commission recommended that ". . . all appointments to, and promotions within, the postal system be made on a non-political basis." But the president of the United States was to appoint the members of the board of directors which would govern the postal establishment; and how could he make a non-political appointment? The national committee of the party in power would certainly assert its influence as would Congress itself.

When Nixon took office, his postmaster general set up yet another survey team in a seemingly endless string of postal reform study groups. But uniquely Winton Blount had the guts—and the backing—to take its advice and cancel some local postmasterships and replace them with out-of-town "officers in charge."

Everyone expects a rescuer to be a knight in shining armor; but the real-life samaritan will probably have mud on his shoes. So it was with the postmaster general when the corporation came into view. Affectionately called "Red," this self-made millionaire came to be called "Bulldozer" Blount. He will always be known as the "blunt" postal general who stamped out some unnecessary local postmasters. His lack of popularity with certain postal people and politicians was exceeded only by his dogmatic stands.

In 1972, five years after the proposal from the predecessor president and his postmaster general, the names are different and our post office is in the throes of change brought about by the great post office debate. Politicians have theorized that little towns like Bean's Corner, U.S.A. will not stay locally oriented, and fear the moguls of big business will not change from being profit-minded to public-minded. While the post office we have known fades into the past, some long for a return to yesteryear.

19.   Legacy of Ills

Postal service needs a continuing analysis. In 1796 a congressional committee was investigating the Post Office. Both Washington and Jefferson complained of the mail service. Trusting one's letter to the U.S. Mail was said to be an act of faith. Two hundred years later, as the postal corporation was about to take over, people having less faith lamented, "Now it's more like playing the odds!"

In 6,100 cities and towns across the nation, more than 180,000 letter carriers served 150,000 routes, making 60 million calls every day. Twenty percent of all Americans moved each year and a simple business transaction like a stock certificate transfer could generate half a dozen letters. Almost a million letters were misdelivered, if less than one percent of the letters went wrong.

That is only part of the picture; seven-eights of the iceberg couldn't be seen. There was a $2 billion postal deficit each year. Of this, $600 million was rightfully chalked up to carrying out the responsibilities designated by Congress as public services. But what about the balance?

Post Office sales now came to $8 billion per year, with only five U.S. businesses surpassing that figure. The Post Office needed imaginative management and to this end established a Bureau of Research and Engineering. Some nine hundred people were scheduled to work in this unit by 1972. Almost a thousand more employees in a new arm was frightening, but mail processing needed to be pushed from horse-and-buggy ways into modern society.

Another farsighted idea of the Postal Service was the Postal Institute. Plans called for this organization to be housed with the Research and Engineering unit. This multimillion dollar project was to be opened in 1972, replete with dormitories for resident students and foreign visitors. Emerging nations are increasingly sending people to this country to learn about postal operations, and the institute would serve them too.

Eventually a staff of three hundred would be required to operate the facility located in Washington, D.C. In addition to the on-campus school, field branches and correspondence courses were planned. It had been a source of chagrin to subordinates and embarrassment to officials when each realized that a supervisor had had no instruction in what could be considered a rudimentary aspect of his job. Of course, the psychological benefit of the schooling was secondary to the tangible savings that were expected to accrue as management became better trained.

Part of the management training was to feature public information. The Post Office was tired of extracting its foot from its mouth. It was getting a little smarter.

A lot had been learned from things like the Turnkey Project. Sixteen million dollars had been spent for an automated "post office of the future" in Providence, R.I.; and it was highly publicized before being fully tested. The whole shebang had been a dismal failure. Before it was scrapped, it was derisively referred to as the "Turkey Project."

Another bad thing for public relations which the new service inherited, was the department's policy of arbitrarily assigning postmarks regardless of locale of posting. This can and does have its consequences. Quite

often taxes are imposed according to mailing addresses.
In many states, cities or townships may annex part of
the surrounding area by showing cause to the courts.
When a housing, industrial or shopping center locates
in an area, the Post Office arbitrarily assigns an office
to process its mail. As the tax base is improved, the city
hall that bears the name of the post office that services
this mail will naturally eye the place with a view to
putting it under their jurisdiction. Their case in court
may be strengthened by the area in question bearing the
same mailing address as the municipality making application for annexation, even though the people in the area
rightfully considered themselves part of another governing area. Probably the discontinuance of traditional postmarks will eliminate this.

Public relations, initiative, good judgment and authority to coordinate postal operations with public practice had been dreadfully lacking in the past. If a business
firm chose to set out a trash container shaped like a mailbox, who was to stop it? How many people have mailed
a letter in a street receptacle plainly marked "Deposit
Litter Here"?

The Post Office was having enough problems of its
own making. Parcel post is typical. Parcels mailed between offices in the United States not designated first
class are allowed to be bigger and heavier than parcels
mailed between first-class offices. Further, in the field of
international mail the United States enters into an individual agreement with every foreign country in the
world. Generally the clerk has to refer to the *Directory
of International Mails* to determine the specific regulations for a particular country. But even with instructions, there has been constant confusion. Let's illustrate
with Canada. According to regulation there is no air
parcel post to Canada; parcels must be sent as letter-class
mail. What happens when a customer wants insurance?
Only parcel post can be insured!

In addition to reviewing regulations, the Postal Service was expected to review its obligations in respect to Constitutional guaranties. The mail service is the only entirely private communication that we have. Although most nations now have a policy that the contents of first-class letters are to be accorded secrecy, we should take pride that basically this is an American concept. During transitory periods of history, the mails were considered fair game for those in power to read. In fact, it was a sovereign right; the rationale was that a government had the right to detect enemies from within as well as without.

At the time of postal change, there had been serious doubts as to whether the American government was securing the mails from the prying eyes of some of its government agents. Although by law, under certain conditions mail has no right to secrecy (several federal statutes forbid the mailing of seditious, treasonous or crime-inciting matter), this is an area where the necessary safeguards should not be relaxed.

The public is, after all, the Post Office's reason for being, but many private citizens averred the Postal Service should be reminded to serve people, as well as big business. They felt the politicians had been bought by moneyed, self-centered users of the mails. Only about twenty percent of all mail is sent by private individuals, yet these same private individuals are a mainstay of the federal treasury; therefore any subsidy to bulk mailers is, in fact, taking money away from private people and giving it to business groups.

Originally, all of the mail handled by our post offices was of a personal nature. As the corporation was coming into being, only about fifty-five percent of the mail was paid at the first class rate; only twenty percent of that personal and the rest business mail. Earlier, a person with something to promote paid a boy to deliver hand-

bills or samples door to door or devised some other way
to get his message across. Now it's all dumped in the
postman's bag.

At the time of the postal changeover one-class mail
was not in the plans. Business was against it. The politicians were against it. Some claimed even the Post Office
was against it. Business wanted the taxpayer to help
pay his postage bill; the politician wanted something to
wrangle with and sell; the Post Office wanted to maintain
and enlarge its bureaucracy. It was charged that there
wasn't a post office that didn't try to do some empire
building. All postal people knew by enlarging their operations, their opportunities for upgrading their own
pay and prestige were enlarged. If so-called junk mail
were to be eliminated, operations would be cut in half.
Everyone was against one-class mail except the private
citizen who paid the bills but had no organization lobbying in his behalf.

In October of 1967, Chairman Monroney of the Senate Post Office and Civil Service Committee had the nerve
to ask the Post Office Department to "develop a paper"
on what would happen if third-class mail was discontinued. Its proponents argued that it generated business
and therefore was good for the economy of a country.
All had to concede that under certain conditions of a
developing economy, that is true. But the United States
had passed that state, according to opponents of the
lower-cost classes. They conceded that mail advertisements were instrumental in raising our gross national
product and standard of living, and that the service was
indispensable and proper at one time; but the same need
no longer existed.

What would have happened if the lower rates of
postage had been discontinued? Although many people
felt that much of the mail being paid at third-class rates
would be sent first-class, representatives of the bulk mail-

ers disagreed. They claimed such legislation would drive them out of business and throw their industry out of work.

Akin to the preceding is the second-class category—newspapers. They however were in a unique position to protect their own interests. Their editorials could openly or subtly foretell grave consequences if the newspaper industry were curtailed by costs of mail delivery. They quoted Justice Holmes: "The use of the mails is almost as much a part of free speech as the right to use our tongues" and concluded their editorials with the plea that no one interfere with their God-given right.

Newspapers got the right to low postage rates before the advent of radio and television because they provided the service of bringing news to the farms. Though the newspaper industry likes to convey the impression that they still operate mainly as a public service, they are in business to make money. Their source of money is paid advertising. Any curtailment of circulation cuts into advertising and ultimately into revenues. The opponents of mail-subsidies for newspapers asked by what authority they continued to reserve or deserve the right to cheaper rates.

Though the Postal Service decided that second and third-class mail was paying for its keep, it was expected that their opponents would be unrelenting in their insistence that ultimately all mail be paid at the first-class rate.

A demon behind some of the ills of the Post Office was an inherited lack of morality on the part of managerial and labor personnel. Shirking duties, abuse of sick leave privileges, unwarranted and unscheduled absences, poor service, lackadaisical attitudes, bad personal conduct—all could be attributed to moral laxity.

National morality has always been a barometer of

the efficiency of government agencies, and post office service is a sure way to take the pulse of not only the patient but the nation. The redeeming feature of the situation is its vulnerability to the desires of the people. Apathy is the breeding ground for almost all ills, but public pressure did bring about change. The nation found no hopeless situations, only men who had become hopeless about them.

The Post Office, historically, had been the arena of a game of deceit oriented towards money; and its largesse had always been a well-stocked larder of political plums. The genesis of the organization had one continuing precept—patronage. This was its Jonah. Our modern day revolutionaries saw only by completely eliminating this could it ever gain proper stature and respect.

With a doomsday forecast, prophets of ultimate extinction equated the postal plight to times when virtues became victims of opportunists. Puritan ethics had been ridiculed. Incentives had been killed. There was no respect for taxpayer money. Every action was mercenary, determined by "what's in it for me?" This was the inherited situation that challenged the new regime.

20. Things Look Up

One would expect a spittoon in the Bean's Corner post office; but it's hard to believe that they were taken out of the post offices of our nation's capital only eighteen years ago. The current generation has never had the privilege of contemplating the oval magnificence of a spittoon, discreetly referred to as a cuspidor, in its day as much a part of the decor and function of a post office as cracker barrels were in the general store.

After I had been working in the Post Office a while, I noticed that only a few of the oldtimers used the spittoons for their original purpose. So, after determining that I was secure in my job, I made an official suggestion that since Andrew Jackson had been dead for 108 years, maybe we could dispense with some of his paraphernalia. I kept in contact with my friend the janitor, who sympathized with my cause; and one day he reported that the spittoon in the superintendent's office was gone.

After the decision that spittoons were expendable had leaked, and the field brass knew they could latch onto some antique brass if they so liked, I was happy to read a directive in the *Postal Bulletin* that henceforth no spittoon would be maintained *at government expense* in any post office. This shut my mouth, modernized the city offices and still allowed fourth-class postmasters and others who would do their own janitorial work to continue having a place to spit in their offices.

Evolution takes a long time. As the corporation concept came into being, it was realized that no great operational change had taken place in the Post Office since the start of zip code—which superseded the old zoning system —in the 60's. Of course, the Postal Savings System had been discontinued on April 27, 1966, but that was not a traumatic action. Its only recent activity had been paying weak interest to people who were either dead or had forgotten their postal savings.

The nation was gravitating towards metropolitan centers, mergers and—some claimed—madness. At the end of fiscal 1969, the number of post offices was down to 32,064, the lowest since 1872; and, America looked forward to whatever postal decision the times might bring. Then, in 1971, everything from the name to the nature of the animal was changed. And there were a multitude of things that needed to be changed.

Suddenly things started happening. Clerks and carriers had long bemoaned the fact that too many of their superiors had never experienced what they, as managers, were expected to supervise. After the changeover, postal management interns were required to case mail, work a distribution rack and walk the streets delivering letters.

In the past the old department interpreted legislation to its own advantage. Bills passed by Congress for the benefit of employees, were interpreted by the department so the intent of the legislators was nullified. Now we began to see examples of the inequities being ironed out.

Employees (other than substitute clerks) whose daily work schedule involved any portion of Sunday were required by law to be paid twenty-five percent additional compensation for that entire day's work. In order to save, post offices had made it a practice to rearrange work schedules so no one got this compensation if it could be avoided. There was a proliferation of substitute clerks scheduled for Sunday work. Regular clerks were scheduled to begin their tour of duty at midnight on Sundays, even though they reported at 10:30 P.M. the rest of the week.

This only appeared to be a savings, because on Monday mornings the regular daylight shift came in at 7 A.M. So between that time and the hour that the night shift went off duty (8:30 A.M. on Mondays), there were the two shifts on duty at the same time—the most unnecessary time for a double shift. Mail volume is typically the lightest of the entire week at the end of the weekend when all in-transit mail has been worked up. That practice was changed by the first labor-management contract with the new Postal Service. It eliminated the category known as substitutes and made them part-time regulars, to have the same benefits regarding Sunday pay, if they had a regular work schedule involving that day.

There was supposed to have been a ratio of five regular clerks for each substitute clerk in the Post Office. Theoretically, the subs were to fill in for absent regulars. It didn't work out that way. Substitutes were a notch lower in job security and different rules applied to them. The regulars stayed on the clock whether there was work for them or not. Subs were so often abused that by the time they were reached on the seniority list and promoted to the regular category, they would think, "Now I will enjoy the status." Just like the oldtimers who said: "I had to put up with such and such, so why shouldn't everybody?"

The Post Office had all kinds of little rules that conflicted and caused dissension. Some could get rather complicated. A regular clerk's workday was shown on his timecard on the day that the majority of service was performed, whereas a substitute's workday was shown on his timecard on the day which his tour of duty started. Therefore for the nightshift beginning before midnight, the regulars hit their timecards on, say, Tuesday, but the substitutes working the same hours were required to hit their cards on the Monday space. Okay. One gets used to that; but every substitute eventually made regular. On that day he would start hitting his timecard one day later. The rules made him come up one day short on his paycheck that week.

A man started his employment as a substitute. As such he was an hourly-rate employee and didn't get any paid holidays. His hourly pay was figured by dividing the annual wages for the position by the number of work-hours in a year (52 weeks times 40 hours per week equals 2,080) less the number of hours in a year for paid holidays (9 holidays of 8 hours each equals 72) which would make 2,080 minus 72 or 2,008. A regular clerk's hourly rate is figured by dividing 2,080 (not 2,008, as a sub) into the annual salary, under the purported reasoning that a regular doesn't work on the holidays but gets the day off. Therefore the substitute got more per hour than a like regular. When they worked the same amount of overtime hours, the substitute, supposedly below the regular in job status, got more money. In fact an employee making regular, a promotion according to departmental personnel forms and propaganda, was therefore getting less per hour.

The labor-management contract signed in July 1971 stipulated that the work force of the major offices would be staffed with ninety percent full-time regular employees and the remainder part-time regulars. In addition, in urban areas employees called outside their normal work week would be given four hours work—not the previous minimum of two.

In some metropolitan areas in recent years there had not been enough job seekers, at the wages offered, to meet the demand, so applicants qualified with lower examination grades. No one thought reducing the requirements was the real answer, but what else could be done? The jobs, ideally, should have been made more desirable. It cuts into morale when some are simply handed something that others had to measure up to. With the corpora-

tion pay increases, job requirements—and morale—
began to be beefed up.

Another bugaboo had been temporary employees.
These workers had not passed the entrance exams for
"certified" employees. Career clerks and carriers often
resented the temporary workers who received and re-
tained their jobs through "the needs of the Service."
The number of temps fluctuated greatly. One year when
it ran around 100,000, the number reached 126,000 at
Christmas time. The annual turnover of temporaries
ranged from fifty to ninety percent. It was an easy semi-
permanent job for students and others who were not
career-oriented to the Post Office. Quite often the only
requirement was a connection. I'll never forget one
seasonal assistant who was almost blind; and he was
assigned to case mail. Another was practically illiterate.
With the new organization, you have faith that similar
situations will not occur again.

Probably the greatest problem is matching personnel
to work. Labor is expensive. It constitutes by far the
greatest expenditure in the budget. A goodly portion of
it has been wasted—either in misguided effort or simple
idleness. No two mail operations are exactly the same.
They may appear so on paper; but closely examined the
differences are great. One of the first things the new
management began was a study of the complexities of
various jobs.

Another step in the right direction was seeking communication with the workers. In July of 1967 the department came out with the first issue of a magazine called
Postal Life, for distribution to every employee. Of course,
it was immediately attacked by the politicos. Rep. Edward J. Derwinski called it a revival of a $160,000 frill,
dropped in an effort to economize. Claiming that the
Post Office was in no better position than it had been, he
asked the budget bureau to investigate. But, thankfully,

the dissemination of information to employees has now increased.

Many mail managers had realized for years that the sensible way to operate the Postal Service would be to do away with the independent post offices in each town and have all units operated as branches of a major geographical or commercial area. Consolidation was seen in the same light as the operation of divisions of private business. It cuts duplication and makes for uniformity and a more efficient total organization.

To a limited extent the new Service accelerated this program. In burgeoning metropolitan areas where further facilities were needed, sectional centers were opened. Career postal managers, without the title of postmaster, were given the jobs of operating the new facilities. When the personnel of the established post offices in that area wanted the new jobs, or when the new facilities siphoned mail from the old offices, the changes were challenged as an invasion of jurisdictions; but to no avail. The complete changeover from a post office for each political division with enough power to swing it to a series of strategically placed operations units will be slow and painful, but nevertheless it is seen as feasible and inevitable.

The Post Office lagged far behind the times. The rules regarding the mailing of intoxicants, for example, forbid any with more than 3.2 percent alcohol in the mails. The next sentence in the *Postal Manual* extended the rule to prohibit "beer, lager beer, ale, porter, wine or other liquors, *regardless* of alcoholic content, when mailed to Indian wards anywhere or into any Indian reservation." Such discrimination was a throwback to the days of subjugation when our Indians were herded into reservations. The law was passed to assist in their containment by denying the "firewater" that might excite them to uprising! One of the first postal reforms—even before the changeover—was a new, slimmer book of regulations. All references to Indian wards was quietly omitted.

One postal paradox had been the over-qualified man delivering mail in the street while an under-qualified one sat in the office as postmaster. This is the essence of what the reorganization was all about. If patronage could be eliminated, the career employees would have more opportunities for advancement.

While some individuals gritted their teeth, many others breathed a sigh of relief when they learned postal headquarters was taking letters of recommendation from congressmen, and returning them, rubber-stamped "In violation of Public Law 91–375."

To expand its managerial flexibility even more, orders were issued that promotions would not necessarily be made from applicants working at a particular office. If no local postal employee was considered qualified for a position that opened, a qualified man from an out-of-town office could be appointed.

Things were happening fast now. Every day's newspaper brought additional postal notes for the public to ponder. Amongst the hullabaloo it was discovered that the ten largest post offices in the country accounted for twenty-one percent of the postal work force! The Magazine Publishers' Association reported their dismay at postage increases. The deadline to pick up the $12 million of unclaimed Postal Savings passed; and Congress gave it to the States. Finally, a fellow out in California stuck a stamp on a hundred dollar bill, attached the addressee's name and address and had it delivered the next day. That's pretty good service!

What about the employees? For the first time in years, every day was exciting!

21.　Stand Up and Salute

Regardless of the cacophony of voices, the changing calendar moved the Post Office into its process of overhaul. The time was finally ripe for a change and the handwriting on the wall was being read. Seldom in history had there been a clearer demarcation between one era and another. Generations of government postmen had carried the messages that had united their nation. Now that work was finished, they asked for no dole—only dignity.

The problems of the Postal Service had not developed overnight and they wouldn't be solved overnight either. The mails had worn shackles too long. One of the chains was political control; the other was administering to two hundred million people with practices set up for twenty million.

The postal politico had played his part and seen to it that the organization had more harness than horse. Unnecessary strapping had been laid on because the Constitution makes no provision to pay political henchmen; but they could be put on the P.O. payrolls. Appointments were finally out of the hands of congressmen, but the pessimists still claimed that political influence can never be completely ignored.

Cynical historians reminded us that it had taken twenty years to get the legislation through Congress. Rep. H. R. Gross of Iowa introduced a bill in 1951, guided by the Hoover Commission, to remove the postmaster general from the cabinet and create an agency called the U.S. Postal Service. But such a delay should not be unexpected. The framers of our Declaration of Independence pointed out that ". . . all experience hath shown that mankind are more disposed to suffer, while evils are sufferable, than to right themselves by abolishing the forms to which they are accustomed."

The ultimate decision, as effected by Congress, was for the Post Office Department to be restructured as an independent establishment in accordance with the provisions of Section 104 of Title 5 of the *United States Code*, which defines independent establishment as "an establishment in the executive branch which is not an Executive department, military department, Government corporation, or part thereof—."

The credit, where credit is due, goes to many people, big and small; many organizations, philanthropic and mercenary. One of the leading organizations in the fight for change was a group known as the Citizens Committee for Postal Reform, its co-chairmen being ex-PMG O'Brien and Thruston B. Morton, the former Republican chairman who served on the post office committees of both House and Senate. They got a lot of pro-corporation information to the public: only American Telephone and Telegraph employs more non-military personnel than the Post Office and only General Motors takes in more money, yet it was costing an average of fifteen dollars a year per taxpayer, in addition to the money he spent for stamps, to cover the operating deficit. After enumerating the ills of the Post Office, they would solicit a monetary contribution for the cause of change.

In addition to dollars from individuals, the Reform Committee was heavily financed by big mailers who raised a kitty of $260,000. The *Congressional Record* for October 9, 1969 shows that $5,000 apiece was contributed by Montgomery Ward, Sears, Roebuck, General Foods, Pitney-Bowes, Procter & Gamble, Time, Inc., Scott Paper, and others.

In June, 1969, the committee sent a letter to various mayors, saying: "Putting the Post Office on a self-supporting basis under charter from Congress will free a billion dollars of our federal budget each year for the urgent social purposes of our times. As a mayor you can understand the urgency of additional funds to channel into urban problems." That, of course, brought charges of hoodwinking.

Many questioned if restructuring was actually necessary. Why couldn't the old management be given the authority to be vested in new management?

Various bills led up to the final draft of H.R. 17070 which was ironed out between the House and Senate in conference. It was sent to President Nixon by a vote of 57 to 7 in the Senate and 339 to 29 in the House. On August 12, 1970 the President signed it into law. The law abolished a department which had been in existence since 1829 and removed the postmaster general from the cabinet. It created the United States Postal Service with the stipulation that it pay its own way. It would be operated by an eleven-man board of governors. Nine members of the board would be appointed by the president with approval of the Senate; and the nine, in turn, would appoint a postmaster general and his deputy. To assist the governing board, the new law provided for a five-man Rate Commission appointed by the president without necessity of Senate confirmation.

More than one thing in the bill was criticized. Mr. Blount, the last postmaster general to enjoy cabinet status and the first of the Postal Service, commented that the chief executive of a $10 billion a year corporation— such as the Post Office—should be paid $200,000 or more annually, not the $60,000 which the new bill allowed. And there was also the charge that the postal lobbies could now concentrate on just five commissioners where they have been lobbying all 535 members of Congress.

An obvious sign of the changes afoot occured on March 11, 1971, when PMG Blount made a business call on the House Post Office Committee and informed the assembled men that he had signed a three-year contract with the Army Corps of Engineers for $1.5 billion of construction. The valiant victor of the struggle for postal reform was able to tell this group things that his predecessors for two hundred years had only been able to ask. The independent postmaster general could march back to his headquarters proudly carrying his shield; not on it as so many had predicted.

Much confusion and nonsense accompanied the postal publicity. Only after the circus was over and the crowd had left, could a realistic appraisal of the situation be made. Those who had claimed that the government mail monopoly was an $8 billion concern that private business wanted, learned in early 1971, that it would soon be a $10 billion organization. This was the budget figure for the Post Office in its reorganized status for fiscal year 1972. The postage rate increase in 1971 accounted for the major part ($1.6 billion) of the gain.

The 1972 budget programmed mail volume at 89.8 billion pieces and employment at 743,944. Total cash income was figured to be $10.3 billion. This included $8.4 billion from mail and service revenues; $164 million from reimbursements for nonpostal services and operating expenses; $250 million from authorized borrowings; $1.5 billion from Congressional appropriation; and $22 million from sale of assets held in a revolving fund.

Of the $1.5 billion of the taxpayers' money requested pursuant to provisions of the Postal Reorganization Act, $934 million was classed a public service subsidy and $481 million was to lighten the burden of increased rates to some mailers during a phasing period of the rate increases.

On May 12, 1971 it was announced that as part of the sweeping changes, the fifteen regional offices would be reduced to five. It would be many years before a significant number of the surplus executives would vacate their positions by deaths, dismissals, resignations and retirements. So part of the program was to offer early retirement to senior regional and headquarters management officials with twenty-five years service or if over fifty years of age with twenty years service. As an incentive for leaving, they were offered a bonus of six months salary. Further, the payment would be withheld until the following January 1, affording a tax break.

About two thousand individuals took advantage of early retirement. The total cost was close to fifteen million dollars. Challenging congressmen were told that the Reorganization Act had taken away their control of pay practices; though the bonus had been offered before the changeover, it would not be paid until after. The Civil Service Commission concurred with the decision. In further defense of the payment it was pointed out that had those who thus retired stayed on the job another year, they would have been paid twice what they got.

Then, in July, came the first collective bargaining between the U.S. government and unions in the history of the nation. The contract signed by the Postal Service and its seven rank-and-file employee unions having exclusive bargaining rights gave the postal workers a pay increase of $1,400 during the first eighteen months of the two-year contract, plus a $300 bonus, payable immediately, for undergoing the corporation changeover.

Although the public had often looked through its picture window and seen the Post Office as a left-footed mail carrier, just as often the person delivering the letters was the most-dedicated, lowest-paid and least-appreciated member of their civil service.

Postology is a profession. It is also a science; it is as exact as mathematics and as inexact as medicine. No one knows all the answers; whoever claims to should be suspect. Romans 1:22 correctly describes the situation: "Claiming to be wise, they become fools."

But probably the best help our mail service could get

would be a strengthening of our moral fiber from the grass roots to the ivory tower. Anything so much "of the people, by the people, and for the people" must necessarily be indicative of the people themselves. It is a shame that the mirrored reflection observed in our postal system became so tarnished.

I would not want to deceive you into thinking that the Post Office could have a religious conversion overnight. I do think, however, that it is high time to pull the wagons in a circle and have the men who are dedicated to the Service stand up and be counted. Those just in for the ride should leave the camp. The pride and the patience of those pulling the load always eventually gets to the breaking point.

We should have whatever postal services the people want, with payment for each made according to the dictates of a democratic process. The postman, representing the federal government, should be allowed to stand erect and tall, proudly proclaiming his and his country's dignity. All of us, like Li'l Abner, should want to salute when the "U.S. Mule" passes by. To do less is to emasculate the man and undermine the might of the federalcy itself.

22.   "It's Just Our Policy!"

It has become something of a national pastime for Americans to criticize their postal system. Complaints resound in the nation's press, reverberate in congressional committees, and are even uttered with chagrin by the president of the United States. Almost every adult in the nation has regular contact with some phase of Post Office operations and its weaknesses and inadequacies quickly come to light. This is not true of other agencies. Probably the main contact a citizen has with the rest of the government is his association with the Treasury Department for tax purposes. And even then, that intercourse is via the U.S. mails.

Exactly what, then, are the troubles and shortcomings that the guardians and patrons of postal service complain about? There comes a time when a standing joke is no more a joke. "When do you expect the 11:30 mail?" can become serious.

A good suggestion program, open to the public as well as the postal personnel, will offer some remedies for the complaints, gripes and contentions. Though many of the Post Office's troubles would tax the wisdom of Solomon, they need to be aired; from suggestions come solutions.

The Postal Service does have a suggestion program but let's compare it with the Ford Motor Company—a big business but not as big as the U.S. Postal Service. This private company, like all successful businesses,

171

knows what makes customer satifaction—progressiveness. Stagnation is the ruination of any business, the
Postal Service included.

To be progressive it is necessary to tap the resources
and inventiveness of all employees. The Ford Motor
Company gives up to one-sixth of the savings which the
company will realize in one year for an adopted suggestion. One year one of their metal and guage checkers won
three top awards, each of $6,000 and a new car for his
suggestions. This man, of course, was the champion sug-
gester of the year, making $18,000 and three new cars in
addition to his $7,000 salary. His ideas saved his em-
ployer $108,000. This was an exceptional case; but it is
an accepted practice in the business world to reward
rank-and-file personnel for their ideas commensurate
with savings.

There is an organization for everything in today's
world—even a National Association for Suggestion Systems, with thirteen hundred member firms. They figure
that in an average year about three million ideas are
submitted to management and the suggestors receive
about $30 million for saving industry about $500 million.
In an average year our government estimates it saves
about $150 million on the 150,000 suggestions that are
adopted.

In recent years postal employees have been submit-
ting upwards of 300,000 suggestions per year, out of
which normally about 50,000 are adopted. These save the
government around $10 million a year, for which it pays
out cash awards totaling about $1 million. This appears
to be a lot of money until you consider that our Post Office
spends $700 million a year on commercial transportation.

When it comes to making changes, our governmental agencies are like preachers who realize it is more
advantageous for those on the West Coast to point out
wrongs in the ways on the East Coast, while those in the

East talk about the West. Preaching, politics and postology from coast to coast are all related.

I don't think that when Ben Franklin willed his spirit of pious conservatism laced with politics to the Post Office, he intended that it be taken overly seriously. He was much too practical for that. Nevertheless, it has been an ingrained tenet of every good (?) government administrator not to risk discarding anything. Whenever a clerk asked if he might do away with an old file, the answer was always, "Yes, as long as you make three copies first!"

The administration of a governmental suggestion program is, by its nature, subject to criticism. Personalities enter in. The system would improve if the identity of those making suggestions was kept confidential until after evaluation. One irate Washington, D.C., postal clerk went so far as to have his lawyer demand a payment of $5,150 which he claimed was owed him for his suggestion to use rubber bands to hold packages of letters together—the idea which Brother Bean found so beneficial.

All kinds of suggestions are sent in. Everything from stamps with beer-flavored glue to zippers around the knees of uniform trousers for conversion to short pants when the weather gets hot! A unique one was to have garbage collectors deliver mail while making their rounds!

In spite of our suggestion program there has been a communication gap that just couldn't be bridged in some areas. Certain rules, regulations, procedures, precedents, customs, etc., were regarded as "policy." Sounding off in this area generally got little recognition. Acceptance of certain suggestions could cause upheavels; and everyone had enough to do without making changes. Therefore many officials, through custom, applied a laissez-faire principle.

It would probably be a waste of time to submit certain suggestions through conventional channels. Only from an outside platform would they be heard. The following pages fall in that category.

The policy of seniority bestowing automatic promotion is sometimes even extended to those employees who could never pass the employee entrance exams. They have been "blanketed-in" by a law that says if an employee performs satisfactorily for a certain period of time he may be given Civil Service status just as if he had passed the entrance exam. There is some reasoning behind this. Some people simply freeze up when it comes to taking a test; these are to be sympathized with. But too many undesirables have also gotten in this way. After all, the exam was designed to separate those who couldn't pass it from those who could.

The postal monopoly—by virtue of being a part of the federal government—has within its reach an untapped reservoir of practically unlimited, economical manpower. This source of labor seethes with unrest, boredom and an unimaginable desire to escape from the confines of unrewarding servitude. The people in our prisons could be trained to do many of the tasks incidental to working the mails.

Studying this suggestion seriously, one appreciates the magnitude of its practical and moral justifications. There are obstacles to overcome but the rewards would justify the efforts. Here are two possibilities which could be developed with many variations, each with a net saving to our government. A special bus could take a trained prison crew to a post office to work some of the more laborious postal jobs. The guard might or might not stay with his charges, depending on the circumstances. Or, the mail could be taken to the inmates rather than the inmates to the mail. Within the confines of the penal complex itself, various menial, time consuming jobs of mail sorting could be performed. Why not give them a chance? At the presentation of the President's Award for Distinguished Federal Civilian Service to the Director of the Federal Bureau of Prisons, those assembled were told that the modern pioneers are "people with the energy and initiative to break through the long accepted boundaries of action." Shall we not pioneer with them?

Within the Postal Service there has too often been a parting of the ways between the advocates of traditionalism and the proponents of modernity. The people in Bean's Corner have been quite willing to continue things in the comfortable manner of yesteryear, but the victims of traumatic changes in urban lifestyles need a society that keeps up with the times. Today the Postal Service must be innovative. "There's no reason; its just our policy" will no longer serve to rebut a suggestion—no matter how far out it seems.

23.   Incentives and Savings

One of the underlying problems with most government service is that it offers too little incentive to its employees. Private industry can provide profit-sharing, company-owned facilities for the use of employees, worker-owned cooperatives, etc. The government, by its nature, is restricted in its ventures for its employees.

However, considering the dire need for incentives, all avenues should be explored. The military have their banking facilities and P.X.'s, so why couldn't other government workers? A federal banking institution could grow from the popular credit unions. It could include investment opportunities, supplemental retirement credits, etc. And why couldn't the Post Office give its employees a year-end bonus commensurate with production increases, crediting this amount to retirement annuities if not applying it annually. The entire purpose of this financial institution would be to provide a stimulus to employees.

Personnel relations could be improved in the smaller offices. They seem to have been by-passed when it comes to having someone to which they may sound off. The postmasters are expected to provide most of the counseling but they cannot rightfully be expected to be an expert in all the many areas of modern personnel work. Then too, quite often an employee is reluctant to go to his direct superior with something that may be looked upon as trivial. He is afraid that it may be construed as a conflict of personalities or reflect on the appellant as a troublemaker. A personnel specialist should be available to the employees of smaller offices, without their having to travel to a distant office for an audience. He should be inconspicuously available and sympathetic towards the employees and present the employee's views to management, as does a sergeant major, the military representative of the enlisted man.

Our use of stamps could be greatly simplified. Many question the need for special stamps for services like special delivery and airmail. Why are airmail stamps acceptable only for articles being airmailed? In the past we have had special stamps for registry, parcel post, newspapers and periodicals. That these have been dropped successfully proves we do not need a special stamp for each different category of service. Why not a single multipurpose stamp?

Did you know that the only valid reason stamps are canceled is because the law requires it? Theoretically, cancellation prevents the reuse of the stamps. When cancellation started, most of the mail was personal and postage was expensive. Now the situation is reversed. The bulk of mail is from the big businesses whose organizational structure is not conducive to cheating on postage, and the postage rates are actually comparatively low. With today's hourly wage rates, hardly anyone could afford to take the time, trouble and chance to lift used postage stamps. Unpeelable musilage could be developed. So is there any use of cancelling low-denomination stamps anymore? Certainly some types and classes of mail could forego this procedure to produce a savings.

On February 1, 1964, the Post Office—in an admitted economy move—discontinued showing the hour of posting on the postmarks. Thereafter they showed only whether the mail was posted in the A.M. or P.M. If this designation was taken out, it would be a further savings. That old watchdog agency, the General Accounting Office, in December 1967 charged that postmarking mail costs money, serves no useful purpose and contributes to the negative side of the debate concerning consolidation of postal facilities and doing away with some of the all-too-many offices. They apparently figured that the further-ance of historical significances and pride in placenames was not a proper function of the Post Office; postal ex-pediency could best be served by a code of origin. If the mails are to be turned into a money-making operation the customers could pay extra for a date-stamp impression.

In recent years we have witnessed the scarcity of metals, especially silver, and the resultant conversion to the sandwich coins with a base metal center. But with the simultaneous advent of so many vending machines taking coins, we are practically forced to continue the standard coins in five, ten and twenty-five cent denomina-tions. What about the half-dollar coins, though? These have several times more metal than the minor ones and as yet their use in vending machines is practically nil. We might consider a form of coin-stamp in lieu of cheap metal half-dollars. Possibly the idea could be extended to other denominations and this would ease certain prob-lems. When you send coins in letters (causing a higher rate of postage) they can fall out of the envelope or tear up the stamp cancelling machines. Coin-stamps, upon being received, could be used as postage or taken to the bank and exchanged for other types of money.

After all, everybody is reconciled to the fact that in our scheme of things we bank more on hope and trust than on hard, concrete value. Any numismatist with a collection of old paper money knows that only the recent bills bear the inscription "In God We Trust." Since the Treasury no longer backs its paper with gold or silver, we have to trust in God. The bills themselves say so! There's a parallel with the Post Office. In the old days people buying a stamp knew they could trust the federal government to send out its Army, if necessary, to protect every bit of the U.S. Mail. Not so anymore; so here too, one has to trust in God!

Another thing that has changed with the times is rural deliveries, formerly known as Rural *Free* Delivery. There are those who say that instead of extending this service, an attempt should be made to curtail or phase it out. Is the cost of this operation in relation to the amount of mail served fair to anyone other than its recipients? The service was established in 1896 when most Americans lived in rural sections in a basically agrarian country. This was before paved highways and automobiles, radio and television. Then the farmer was isolated in a way which our modern farmer would find hard to imagine.

Rural delivery was started as a service to the secluded and was originally called the *Farmer's Free Delivery*. It has never paid its way, which was all right back then; but how many of the present-day rural patrons are farmers? Even so, about the only connection these few farmers have with the requirements of those of the previous generations is nostalgia.

There are about 31,000 rural carriers on the federal payroll; and over 37 million people, or roughly twenty percent of all Americans, receive their mail from them. This represents over ten million families. Their routes collectively approximate four round-trips to the moon daily. As of this writing, the shortest route, at Blue Island, Ill. is 4.3 miles and the longest, at Poplarsville, Miss. is 158.2 miles; the nationwide average is 65 miles. Many carriers finish their routes early and devote the major part of the day to secondary (?) jobs. With rural routes costing our nation over $400 million annually, many urban citizens question why they should help pay for this expensive service.

The post offices would be money ahead by giving lock boxes, for which they at present charge a rental fee,

to those who would accept them in lieu of having a rural
carrier deliver their mail. Possibly the boxes could be set
up in a convenient local place—bank, library or community kiosk.

The General Accounting Office consistently urged
the Post Office Department to quit paying rural carriers
for the use of their personal vehicles and instead supply
official ones. The comptroller general annually urged
Congress to permit this. Savings of about thirty million
dollars per year were projected. But since the carriers
got 12¢ per mile or $4.20 per day, whichever is greater,
as compensation for driving their personal vehicles, they
and their unions categorically opposed any reduction in
the use of private vehicles.

The situation is about the same concerning fourth
class offices, those with gross annual receipts of about
$2,000 or less as determined by a complicated formula
involving various entries in the cashbook. The offices of
Naylor and Hall, in Prince Georges County, Maryland—
one of the highest per capita income counties in the nation—had total receipts in a recent year of only $970 and
$587, respectively. Many other places have shown annual
receipts of only $100 per year. We have some 8,400 of
these little institutions. Many are still being operated
much as Abe Lincoln did when he was postmaster, and
said that he "carried the office around in his hat."

In a Sunday afternoon's drive you can come across
them hidden in the byways of semi-rural America. They
are in general stores, homes, gasoline stations or simple
shacks along the road, with a sign in any color, shape or
size, proclaiming their distinction. About the only thing
that they have in common is *Post Office* is always spelled
correctly, thanks to periodic checks by the Inspection
Service. These facilities quite often are a touch of genuine
Americana—a living throwback to a bygone era.

The postmaster's salary is about fifteen hundred dollars. He provides the space and the government pays him

rent for the quarters: a simple arrangement, designed for convenience. Regulations have been known to be stretched a little in order to keep everyone happy. The Post Office Department had to have the sanction of the area's representative to discontinue any of these offices; and the congressman might've been cutting off the hand that fed him if he took the postal income from the local political heeler. Until reorganization, the postmaster had to die, resign or retire before the office was closed; and even then the shutdown had to be cleared through the congressman.

Being in the employ of the government is unlike that of private business because within governmental offices there can be no function outside the scope of a predetermined wall of authority. Legal, democratic processes dictate no provision for a latitude in operations. This restrictive situation often makes a civil-service employee feel stymied and frustrated. Therefore, the favorite pastime of many postal workers within a few years of optional retirement is the counting of the months, weeks and days until that dreamed-of Utopia, the promised land of milk and honey, replete with a rocking chair and fishing pole. This great American dream is made possible financially through the liberalization of the Civil Service Retirement System.

In reality it is still only a dream though, because most men are not made for this kind of life. To be complete, a man has to be gainfully occupied. An experience of one man I know typifies many. To make himself useful he began to accompany the local church kindergarten, in which his wife was a teacher, on their field trips. One day he overheard a little girl ask her playmate why Mr. X always went with them. Her little friend, confused by the state of retirement, answered, "I think it has something to do with him being retarded!"

Why bring up retirement? Because the government, especially the Post Office which by its nature is so amenable to part-time employment, could very well use many of their retired employees to the advantage of both the government and the retirees. A special catgeory could be set up. Then workers could ease out of full-time employment with a better outlook and the government needn't completely lose their skills.

All occupations have their various idiosyncrasies and problems. Just what are they for postal people? It would take an in-depth study by trained occupational specialists to determine them. This information could certainly be beneficial to the Postal Service.

Our records show that ten thousand postmen suffer dog bites each year with five percent of them requiring hospitalization or other medical care. What our records don't show is the subtly psychological makeup of these men. It would seem that a country which could spend $13,500 to study the behavior of monkeys in the Caribbean could afford at least a like amount for the *homo sapiens* who deliver their mail.

24.   Washington's Smallest Room: P.O.D. Hall of Fame!

We old farmers running the Post Office had been in the habit of tieing it up with baling wire, hoping to get through another season. But the general store was going out of business; and we couldn't find baling wire anymore. It was time to take more positive measures. Luckily, a man named Kappel—whom history should recognize as *the* modern-day postal reformer—was framing a new postal picture.

The sad situation of our mails was brought about by the proliferation of things that were individually minute but collectively constricted the heart of the organization. Inherited inefficiency coupled with the modern laxity took its toll.

Bringing about some semblance of uniformity among offices, personnel and services was the first order of business. Inconsistencies were as firmly cemented in postal services as the mortar and stone of the post office buildings themselves. And the postal abodes demonstrated that. Some offices appeared to be awaiting court receivership while in the next village the post office would be located in the best building in town: one built by the W.P.A. in 1939.

Individually, some of the facilities were efficient, but managing them collectively was like streamlining a tangle of spaghetti. It was a big job just trying to unravel the mess, to keep the bad offices from strangling the good ones.

About the only thing the offices had in common was the U.S. flag out front giving each the imprimatur of official Americana. A building displaying a flag means a post office to many. On July 14, when banking institutions among others, celebrate Flag Day by displaying the Stars and Stripes, there are always some in the cities who come in to deposit mail (not money).

Individuals showed the same inconsistencies as the offices. But, the good guys didn't wear white hats and the bad boys black ones; they worked side by side. The good guy might have saved many a day and never been given recognition. A bad boy might have pilfered a package and taken letters containing cash. He might even have been a member of a gang of petty thieves who slapped their own address labels over the rightful ones, having whatever was wanted delivered at Uncle Sam's expense wherever they wanted it. About the only deterrent was conscience.

Some personnel, as an approach to consistency in services, were advocating single category mail, travelling by the fastest available means. They based their suggestion on the laws considering any mail—first, second, or third class—to be a letter. In this vein, Postmaster General O'Brien asked Congress in 1968 to abolish domestic airmail and airmail stamps, and have all first-class mail flown, if and when flying would advance it. The elimination of the segregation by air and surface would effect savings. Most of the nation's first-class letters were airlifted anyway, being loaded on planes having vacant space with a reduced rate charged for their haulage.

In a continuing effort to streamline the mail mess, the Post Office Department developed a number of alphabet plans. (See Acronyms: Appendix D.) The lower echelons of postal employees said; "You can't get the mail worked just by talking about it," but this word apparently never reached the higher strata who felt that by minting a name they could move the mail.

In spite of all the phraseology, history has shown that many technological advances come from the public. A nineteen-year-old girl in Oregon, who was never a postal worker, designed and applied for a patent on an envelope which is unique in that it has a one-inch by three-inch section in the upper lefthand corner, perforated for easy removal and gummed on the back. The addressee can detach the gummed label showing the sender's address, and use it as a stick-on address for a reply communication. Her idea would curtail errors in copying and could permit electronic sorting of the return letter which otherwise might be handwritten.

In 1971 the administrators decided they had better take lessons from postal history. The postmaster general created an office to which the general public could send their complaints and suggestions. Write to Ombudsman, Postal Service Headquarters, Washington, D.C. 20260.

There are a number of changes in the works for the near future. We have already seen the overprinting of postage stamps with an invisible luminescent ink that activates ultraviolet sensing devices on automated cancelling machines to speed mail sorting. This and the use of magnetic ink; the kind used by banks on checks, will be expanded. There will be widespread use of self-service postal units. Their cost per transaction is proven to be only half what it would be at a post office window. The number and services of businesses specializing in message delivery will expand. Although the government has a monopoly on the delivery of mail, the post office's attitude toward protecting this has been ambivalent.

The postal reformists of late did not see fit to enfranchise private carriers. And no organization in this country, except the U.S. Mail is allowed to deliver a letter

without permission. Under the Private Express Statute of 1936, a letter is defined as "a message in writing from one person to another containing live, current information which would incite the recipient to act or to refrain from answering." Further, it need not be in handwriting; it can be in any language or code. It may simply be a series of printed letters, punched holes or raised characters. The intent of the description is to cover all recorded messages between people.

Why then can business firms specializing in the transportation and delivery of mail (e.g. United Parcel Service) enjoy such a boom? To what extent will the Postal Service enforce their monopoly? They seem to feel if private business can do a job to the customer's satisfaction, why not permit it? On the other hand, the government provides certain services that private business could not, or would not want to do. This precludes free enterprise from taking over the entire operation.

Some argue that private concerns should be allowed to assume all the delivery business they can since our government post is prone to operate at a deficit. The more business others do, the less government money is lost. Surely cost and quality have entered into the public's choice of service which made the private entrepreneurs successful; so government necessarily bows to its constituency. But there is counter opinion that private business interests have always wanted to get the postal service into their hands; and wary individuals feel that the moguls of industry are even less perfect than the government. Private enterprise must be watched to ensure that all people are served and not just the profitable ones.

Logistics is one of the consistent post office problems. Most postal buildings were built in the center of cities near railroad depots in a time when trains carried the mails. Now we need them at the airports. The problem is compounded by 92 percent of all mail being handled in the big cities. Transportation experts have considered planes with vertical or short take-off and landing capabilities, helicopters and high-speed rail systems to bypass congestion between cities and suburbs.

And while straightening things out, why not meld telephone area codes and zip codes? At present, neither have any geographical significance. With some uniformity, they both would. All public service organs should cooperate to develop a system that would have the most beneficence to the overall plan.

The ever increasing amount of mail being handled has made ever increasing demands for cheaper, more efficient and faster mail sorting. Perhaps it's not the ultimate solution but in 1969 a group of Russian scientists proposed that pigeons be put to work as sorters. The scientific journal *Zwaniye* ("knowledge is strength") reported that pigeons can read—they can differentiate among all thirty-three letters in the Russian alphabet. "If letters are used as a sort of code for zones, a line of thirty-three pigeons, each trained to spot one letter, could sort the mail according to its zone," the magazine said. And further, "All honest labor must be paid for, so from time to time a grain falls from a feeder and lands at the pigeon's feet." Perhaps a new kind of "pigeon post" is in the offing.

More expensive, but undoubtedly faster, is the letter sorting machine. With this, an operator is expected to process 30,000 to 36,000 letters per hour with 98 percent accuracy, approximating one letter per second—twice the production of clerks processing letters in the conventional manner. A $6 million contract was let in 1966 with Burroughs Corp. for 53 of these machines. They are 77 feet long, weigh 15 tons, stand 9.5 feet high and cost $115,000 each. In 1971 some 150 of these machines were being operated.

Since the nation's 74 largest post offices handle 52

percent of all the mail, these highly concentrated areas warrant some costly, sophisticated devices that would not be economically feasible in other places.

Banks have read account numbers by machine for quite some time. But their situation was simpler than the Post Office's. Their forms are standardized, with only one typeface (some 600 fonts are in use in this country) and the printing to be read is located in only one position. Now, thanks to private industry, there is an electronic sorter that is applicable to the mails. It is a robot reader with an electrical impulse which is altered according to the contrast between one color (the writing) and another color (the envelope). At present this machine can do a fair job of reading letters and combinations of letters. Upon determining the addresses on mail mechanically fed into it, the machine routes the letters into their respective channels, making a different separation for rejects to be read by humans. It takes no stretch of the imagination to visualize this machine reading zip codes. No doubt it will someday be perfected to the point of reading legible, cursive writing.

Many of the concepts of providing mail service in the future are rightfully grounded on the premise that private businesses and research corporations will perfect inventions for use by the new Postal Service. Government owned concerns cannot profit from by-products of their own research, therefore the cost of extensive governmental research is prohibitive.

In September of 1969 the postmaster general awarded a $147,046 contract for a state-of-the-art study of electronic communication techniques to General Dynamics of San Diego, Calif. It suggested messages being conveyed electronically to post offices, converted to hard copy and delivered to the customers. This could eventually lead to the use of home receivers which print facsimiles, and offer an alternative to the physical carrying of the mails. The letter carrier as the people know him today may become as rare as a cigar-store Indian.

A numeric speech translator is being developed which will convert spoken numbers into machine instructions. As mail is carried on a conveyor past the clerk, he speaks the first three numbers of the zip code, which tells the distribution point to which the mail should be directed. Experimental equipment has been tested with recorded spoken numbers by 250 employees in cities selected to include geographic differences in speech.

Amongst other revolutionary communication innovations is the laser beam, still in its infancy but promising to bring startling changes to the transmission of messages. Practical, working scientists of the major communication combines concede that it will, in time, be commonplace to transmit messages on these beams of light, without the wires and cables needed today. A form of "instant wire" that transmits color, but is actually an invisible beam, has been developed by British scientists.

Now that we have seen what television can do—and only 25 years ago it was where laser research is today— it would not be far fetched to visualize equally remarkable advances in this new field. Why not beam pictures (letters) and have the receiver re-create the object on paper, to a depth of detail beyond that of human eyesight? I have no doubt that this will be in the postal service of the future.

Would you believe that a super V-mail may be on the verge of a comeback? Its only negative side is the patron's lack of confidence that no one will violate his privacy by reading his message. With today's microminiaturization, many pounds of printed matter can be reduced and put on an ounce of film. Capsules containing these could be shot toward their destinations, like a rocket, then homed in to the receiving office as military missiles are guided to the target.

The most caustic postal critics say many of these projects could already have become reality if it were not for the inefficiency and lack of progressiveness in the Post Office Department. The most harsh contend the smallest room in Washington is the P.O.D. Hall of Fame —it had the only appropriated money in history that our government couldn't get rid of! It is even jokingly said that the only candidate for occupancy—Ben Franklin— is largely noted for talking about lightning mail-delivery while flying a kite during office hours!

But we who have spent decades laboring alongside the old post office horse, hope that history will treat us more kindly. Our generation, born before and during the Depression, arrived in time to see two worlds, neither small. We inherited the holdovers of early America, changed them with the challenge of a modern world—and got crushed in the middle.

Appendices

A. Chronology of Postal Landmarks

4,000 B.C.: Indications are that an organized message delivery service existed in the civilization of the Indus Valley, now part of India and Pakistan.

3,800 B.C.: The Louvre in Paris has clay seals of this date, used as stamps on letters delivered in Babylon.

3,000 B.C.: Messages written in hieroglyphics on papyrus and fabric were sent through the Egyptian Kingdom.

1,500 B.C.: Egyptian tomb inscriptions refer to a letter delivery service.

700 B.C.: Biblical translations mention King Hezekiah's postal system which extended throughout Israel and Judeah.

500 B.C.: The writings of Confucius mention post offices.

400 B.C.: There exist reference to the Greeks' postal system of this time.

60 B.C.: The Roman Empire under Julius Caesar inaugurated a courier system and official post that kept the government in contact with the far-flung military outposts.

200 A.D.: By this date, the Persian and Roman empires had highly developed official posts.

300: Diocletian, Roman Emperor 284–305, established the first postal service in Europe open to private persons.

1100: Kublai Khan established an efficient postal system in China which lasted about 600 years.

1200: The University of Paris organized receipt and delivery of mail for its students. The University was paid a compensation in 1719 when the government took over this service.

1216: Beginning of documentary evidence of English postal system.

1400: Mail was being carried in Mexico by the Aztecs.

1460: First postmarks used about this time.

1460: Roger of Thurn und Taxis was granted rights to operate a post between the Tyrol and the Italian States.

1464: Louis XI of France established for his court, the first approximation to our modern post. During the reign of his son Charles VIII, this was opened to the public on a space available basis.

1519: A letter mailed to Leonardo da Vinci in this year, with a handstruck postmark, still exists.

1530: Henry VIII established a postal organization which became the basis of the present English system and the model for all other European countries. His postmaster general Sir Brian Tuke is the first about whom there is documentary evidence.

1591: Queen Elizabeth I prohibited the transportation of letters of "Countreys Beyond the Seas" except by authorization of the Crown. This was designed to stop the private posts of the foreign merchants, bring in revenue, and provide censorship—all then considered the right of a ruler.

1632: Thomas Witherings and William Frizell purchased the English postal service concession to foreign parts. Witherings was the first of a line of English postal reformers. He established postal rates based on distance and devised a system of main postal lines with major distribution points at the terminus of each. He increased and speeded communications with the continent through a contract with the house of Thurn und Taxis. The fees he charged for "portage" were the forerunners of "postage" charges and the word itself thus derived.

1639: On Sept. 5 the General Court of Massachusetts, designated Boston socialite Richard Fairbanks the first postmaster in the colonies.

1643: France had parcel post as well as letter post in operation.

1653: In July of this year, Louis XIV gave the Comte de Nogent and Sieur de Villayer the right to operate a post in Paris. They created the first postal paper, a ticket marked postage paid showing proper prepayment of postage. M. de Villayer, the active partner, invented a wrapper with appropriate markings, in which his patrons could enclose their letters. He also set up mail boxes in which patrons could drop letters enclosed in these wrappers, with the idea that they would be collected and delivered by his carriers. His venture was not successful and his idea for showing prepayment of postage soon forgotten.

1657: The Post Office of England was created. A federal monopoly, it made postal service available to anyone. There were extensive provisions regarding postage rates.

1657: The Colonial Court of Virginia required every planter to convey official dispatches to the next plantation under penalty of fine. By 1661 the Virginia

Assembly required "all letters superscribed for the service of His Majesty or publique" be forwarded.

1661: Postmaster General Henry Bishop of England invented a date stamp device with which to postmark mail.

1683: A post route from Maine to Georgia was opened.

1692: On Feb. 17, the British government authorized Thomas Neale to set up a national postal service in the American colonies.

1711: The various private posts in England were consolidated with the royal messenger service into a central organization.

1755: Mail began to be dispatched between the Colonies and England on a monthly schedule.

1766: In Mexico a mail delivery system was established by the Spanish governors.

1772: Vienna possessed a local letter post and parcel post on a prepayment plan.

1784: On August 2, the first mail coach, supplanting foot and horsemen, was introduced in England by John Palmer. It began a run from Bristol to London.

1785: On Jan. 7, French balloonist Pierre Blanchard and an American physician Dr. John Jeffries made a balloon flight from Dover, England to De Felmores, France carrying the first mail by air in a man-made vehicle.

1789: A postal service was duly authorized by the U.S. Congress on Sept. 22.

1811: A Scottish shipping line used adhesive stamps for its private postal service—probably the first widespread use of postage stamps and a contributing factor to their eventual official use.

1818: In November the Sardinian postal ministry put stamped writing paper, known as carta postale bollata or Sardinian covers, on sale. A watermark was used to prevent forgery.

1830: The first railway mail was sent from Liverpool, England, to Manchester on November 11.

1834: James Chalmers, a printer in Dundee, Scotland, designed and printed a gummed experimental stamp, one of the first "adhesives" in philately.

1836: U.S. Congress passed an act forbidding mail to be withheld from anyone. This was precipitated because of previous incidents of denying mail to opposing political factions.

1838: In November the British dominion of New South Wales sold the first letter sheets having embossed designs indicating prepaid postage.

1839: February 20 is the date shown on an Austrian letter bearing a stamp. When this letter was found in 1952 some adjudged its stamp the first—antedating the Penny Black of 1840. Finally it was figured the stamp was unofficial; devised by the postmaster of Spittal, Austria, in an attempt to collect the standard, though voluntary, remuneration of one kreuzer for the delivery of a letter.

On August 27th, England made postal reforms which greatly improved service. Rates were figured on weight, not distance, and paper bags marked to show that the postage had been paid, were authorized for enclosure of letters.

1840: On May 1 first postage stamps and wrappers were offered for sale in England, for use beginning the sixth of the month. The letter sheets and envelopes called Mulreadys, for their designer London artist William Mulready, died aborning. Conversely, the sticky stamps were an instantaneous success.

1840: Stamps were issued by the postmasters of Alexandria, Baltimore, New Haven, New York, and St.

Louis. They were known as Postmasters Provisionals, had no federal warranty, and were used only locally.

1841: Blood's Dispatch, in Philadelphia, issued the first private postage stamp in the United States.

1843: In March the Canton of Zurich became the second place in Europe to issue stamps (after England) and the first on the Continent. In July Brazil came to be the first government in the Western Hemisphere to do so, and the second in the world.

1845: On December 1 Russia introduced stamped envelopes, or letter sheets. Originally for the use of the nobility, they were soon allowed for everyone.

1854: In Ireland Henry Archer invented a perforation machine for stamps. While passing the time over a glass of ale, he noticed a journalist use his stick pin to separate stamps from a sheet, and developed his machine from this man's ingenuity.

1855: Pillar type letter boxes were introduced in London, England. Prepayment of postage became compulsory in the United States.

1857: In the United States, the first patent for a postmarking and stamp cancelling machine was granted.

1859: On July 1, the balloon *Atlantic* became the first aircraft to carry mail in the United States. The flight from St. Louis to New York City ended near Henderson, New York, after the mail had been thrown overboard. But it was recovered and delivered undamaged.

1860: Pony Express started on April 3 between St. Joseph, Mo. and Sacramento, Calif.

1865: M. de Velayer, operating a postal service in Paris, sold stamps printed on isinglass for the prepayment of postage. These articles, known as *billets port paye*, became collectors items.

1869: Austria became the first country to introduce the post card. It was adopted in England the following year.

1870: The Franco-Prussian War tested the ingenuity of French postmasters. With Paris under seige, a pigeon post was first tried. Then on the 26th of September, balloon service was inaugurated. Fifty-seven of sixty-seven ascents were successful; and only five balloons were captured. Letters carried by balloon were marked *"Par Balloon Monté."*

1874: The Universal Postal Union (originally General Postal Union) was founded at Bern, Switzerland, enabling uniformity in transmission and delivery of mail throughout the world.

1878: International parcel post was established at the Postal Union Congress in Paris.

1890: A world postage stamp was advocated by Siegmund Friedl, editor of the magazine *World Post.* This idea keeps cropping up.

1892: In July the pneumatic tube between Berlin and Paris carried letters between these two cities in thirty five minutes.

1897: The first semipostal (charity) stamps were issued by New South Wales. The overage of price above face value went to a home for "consumptives."

1902: Postage meters originated in New Zealand.

1911: In August, Jules Vedrines flew letters from Paris to Deauville, the first carried by plane.
 In the United States, the first airmail flight took place on Sept. 23 when Earle L. Ovington flew from Garden City, to Mineola, N.Y.

1918: First regular airmail service in the world started Mar. 20; Vienna to Kiev. The first scheduled airmail flight in the United States inaugurating regular air delivery between Washington, D.C. and New York City, took place on May 15.

1948: Air Parcel Post was inaugurated in the United States and between Europe, South America and the U.S. territories and possessions.

1969: On July 20 Astronaut Neil A. Armstrong canceled the first piece of mail on the moon with the slogan "Moon Landing, U.S.A." This was the longest mail run in history.

B.   Postmasters General

Although we have had six presidents from the State of Virginia, no citizen of that state has served as postmaster general. Since we have been a nation, the postmasters general have had fifty-seven different names. There have been no Jones and only one Smith. Only two surnames have been repeated: Brown and Granger. Outstanding for his given name is PMG Return J. Meigs, Jr. He—so it is said—got it because of his grandfather's courtship. After a rejected proposal, his intended suddenly called, "Return, Jonathan," and consented to marriage. In jubilant remembrance, the offspring from that union was named Return Jonathan. His son Return, Jr., was our fifth postmaster general.

When W. Marvin Watson was appointed postmaster general, he was hailed by the press as the sixty-first to hold the office. I calculated him number fifty-eight. My curiosity aroused, I wrote to the department and received Form PL-20, a list of all postmasters general. Apparently this was where the press got their wrong number. The list included the three provisional appointees of the Continental Congress. The first two were appointed before the Colonies even declared themselves self-governing! The third before the office of Postmaster General of the United States was created by the Act of September 22, 1789 (1 Stat. 70).

Ben Franklin is traditionally thought of as the first Postmaster General of the United States. He was a postmaster general but his title was conferred by the Crown before the independence of the Colonies. Samuel Osgood was the first Postmaster General of the United States. Clinching my claim that Franklin should not be recognized as the first postmaster general is the fact that the Continental Congress also appointed a president, John Hanson. He is not officially recognized as the first, so why should Franklin be?

Legal heads of British Colonial Postal Matters in America prior to Appointment of a Postmaster General:

Name	Date of Appointment	Position Held
1 Thomas Neale	1691	Patent for twenty-one years from King William
2 Andrew Hamilton	1699	Patent assigned by Neale
3 John Hamilton	1707	Deputy Postmaster General

(The Crown purchased the patent from deceased Andrew Hamilton's business successors and then appointed his son, John, who served until 1730.)

Postmasters General of the Colonies appointed by Crown of England:

Name	Date of Appointment
1 Alexander Spotswood	1730
2 Head Lynch	1739
3 Elliot Benger	1743

Name	Date of Appointment
4 Benjamin Franklin (joint)	1753
5 William Hunter (joint)	1753
6 John Foxcroft (joint) (succeeding deceased Hunter)	1761

Continental Congress Appointees

Name	Date of Appointment
1 Benjamin Franklin	1775
2 Richard Bache	1776
3 Ebenezer Hazard	1782

Postmasters General of the United States and Significant Events

Name	Date of Appointment	Appointed By
1 Samuel Osgood	1789	Washington

The United States had a population of three million not counting slaves and Indians.

2 Timothy Pickering	1791	Washington
3 Joseph Habersham	1795	Washington
Joseph Habersham	continued	J. Adams
Joseph Habersham	continued	Jefferson

When he took office, the department consisted of himself, an assistant and three clerks. He added three more clerks.

Name	Date of Appointment	Appointed By
4 Gideon Granger	1801	Jefferson
Gideon Granger	continued	Madison

Served longest of any postmaster general.

| 5 Return J. Meigs, Jr. | 1814 | Madison |
| Return J. Meigs, Jr. | continued | Monroe |

Under him, the post roads were extended into the wilderness as a means to develop the nation.

| 6 John McLean | 1823 | Monroe |
| John McLean | continued | J. Q. Adams |

The Dead Letter Office was established.

| 7 William T. Barry | 1829 | Jackson |

The first postmaster general to have cabinet status. Prior to this they served in the Treasury Department.
He resigned under Congressional charges of inefficiency and corruption.

| 8 Amos Kendall | 1835 | Jackson |
| Amos Kendall | continued | Van Buren |

The official seal of the Post Office Department was adopted.

9 John M. Niles	1840	Van Buren
10 Francis Granger	1841	W. H. Harrison
Francis Granger	continued	Tyler
11 Chas. A. Wickliffe	1841	Tyler
12 Cave Johnson	1845	Polk

Stamped envelopes were adopted and the first officially authorized U.S. stamps were issued.

| 13 Jacob Collamer | 1849 | Taylor |
| 14 Nathan K. Hall | 1850 | Fillmore |

Flat postage rates of three cents for letters weighing no more than a half ounce and going no more than three thousand miles were inaugurated. Fee for longer distances was six cents.

Name	Date of Appointment	Appointed By
15 Samuel D. Hubbard	1852	Fillmore
16 James Campbell	1853	Pierce

Stamped envelopes first issued. Postal volume doubled during his tenure attributable to lower postage rates and the use of adhesive postage stamps.

17 Aaron V. Brown	1857	Buchanan

Street letter boxes adopted.

18 Joseph Holt	1859	Buchanan

First mail transported by lighter-than-aircraft (balloon). Star Route contract service was started.

19 Horatio King	1861	Buchanan

First career postal employee to become postmaster general. But was appointed only for the final month of President Buchanan's administration.

20 Montgomery Blair	1861	Lincoln

Money order system started. The railway mail service inaugurated and free city delivery began. The International Postal Union was organized.

21 William Dennison	1864	Lincoln
William Dennison	continued	A. Johnson
22 Alexander W. Randall	1866	A. Johnson
23 John A. J. Creswell	1869	Grant

Postal cards were adopted.

24 James W. Marshall	1874	Grant
25 Marshall Jewell	1874	Grant
26 James N. Tyner	1876	Grant
27 David McK. Key	1877	Hayes
28 Horace Maynard	1880	Hayes
29 Thomas L. James	1881	Garfield
Thomas L. James	continued	Arthur
30 Timothy O. Howe	1881	Arthur

Name   Date of Appointment   Appointed By

31   Walter Q. Gresham   1883   Arthur
     First Civil Service bill passed. It required competitive ex-
     aminations for letter carriers and clerks in all offices having
     as many as fifty employees.

32   Frank Hatton   1884   Arthur
33   William F. Vilas   1885   Cleveland
     Special Delivery, stamped newspaper wrappers, and en-
     velopes bearing a request for return if not delivered, were
     started. Towns of 10,000 population became eligible for free
     delivery.

34   Don M. Dickinson   1888   Cleveland
     Railway mail clerks came under Civil Service.

35   John Wanamaker   1889   Harrison
     Issued the nation's first commemorative postage stamp.
     Started front door letter boxes delivery. The first "Post
     Office on Wheels" made its maiden run in Carroll County, Md.

36   Wilson S. Bissell   1893   Cleveland
     The job of printing postage stamps was given to the Bureau
     of Engraving and Printing.

37   William L. Wilson   1895   Cleveland
     Started Rural Free Delivery.

38   James A. Gary   1897   McKinley
39   Charles E. Smith   1898   McKinley
     Charles E. Smith   continued   T. Roosevelt
     First stamp booklets printed.

40   Henry C. Payne   1902   T. Roosevelt
41   Robert J. Wynne   1904   T. Roosevelt
42   George B. Cortelyou   1905   T. Roosevelt
43   George Von L. Meyer   1907   T. Roosevelt
     Coil stamps started.

Name	Date of Appointment	Appointed By

44 Frank H. Hitchcock   1909   Taft
Postal Savings started. First airmail service.

45 Albert S. Burleson   1913   Wilson
He is generally held in disfavor as a union-buster; however many innovations were introduced in his administration: insured mail service, parcel post, C.O.D. and postage meters.

46 Will H. Hays   1921   Harding
Airmail service was extended to include a transcontinental route.

47 Hubert Work   1922   Harding
48 Harry S. New   1923   Harding
       Harry S. New   continued   Coolidge
Special handling service offered for the first time.

49 Walter F. Brown   1929   Hoover
U.S. Airmail Flag adopted for display on buildings handling airmail.

50 James A. Farley   1933   F. D. Roosevelt
First trans-Pacific airmail service established between San Francisco and Manila via the "China Clipper."

51 Frank C. Walker   1940   F. D. Roosevelt
       Frank C. Walker   continued   Truman
Highway Post Offices began. Postal Zoning System started.

52 Robert E. Hannigan   1945   Truman
53 Jesse M. Donaldson   1947   Truman
One of two postmasters general to come up through department ranks. The other served only a lame-duck term. World-wide parcel post inaugurated.

54 Arthur Summerfield   1953   Eisenhower
The Airlift Program, Certified mail and Combination mail began.

Name	Date of Appointment	Appointed By
55 J. Edward Day	1961	Kennedy

His administration brought about union recognition, whereby postal management would have to negotiate with postal unions regarding working conditions, etc. Precanceled postcards authorized.

56 John A. Grounouski	1963	L. B. Johnson

Zip Code program started. Luminescent (tagged) stamps first used. Use of hour of postmark in cancellations discontinued.

57 Lawrence F. O'Brien	1963	L. B. Johnson
58 W. Marvin Watson	1968	L. B. Johnson
59 Winton M. Blount	1969	Nixon

Mailgram, combination letter-telegram, started. Effected the most comprehensive postal reorganization in the history of the nation. Was last postmaster general to be appointed by a president and the first of the new Postal Service.

60 Elmer T. Klassen	1972	Board of Governors, U.S.P.S.

The Confederate States of America, 1861–1865

Name	Date of Appointment	President
1 Henry T. Ellett	1861	J. Davis
2 John H. Reagon	1861	J. Davis

C.   Inaugural Dates of U.S. Postal Services

Certified mail introduced June 6, 1955.

City delivery (free) authorized by act of March 3, 1863. Established July 1, 1863.

COD service inaugurated July 1, 1913, under act of Congress of August 24, 1912.

Highway post office started Feb. 10, 1941.

Insurance service inaugurated July 1, 1855, under act of March 3, 1855.

Money order system went into operation on Nov. 1, 1864, under act of Congress of May 17, 1864.

Newspaper wrappers first issued under act of Feb. 27, 1861. Not made after Oct. 9, 1934.

Parcel post started in the United States on Jan. 1, 1913.

International parcel post had begun in 1878. Air parcel post, domestic and international, started in 1948.

Postage stamps placed on sale at New York, N.Y. on July 1, 1847 under act of March 3, 1847.

Postal cards first issued May 1, 1873, under act of June 8, 1872.

Savings system inaugurated Jan. 3, 1911, under act of June 25, 1910. No new accounts accepted after April 27, 1966, when all interest on Postal Savings ceased under Public Law 89–377.

Railway mail service inaugurated in 1864, after having been operated experimentally since July of 1862.

Registered mail began on July 1, 1855, under act of March 3, 1855.

Rural delivery service established on an experimental basis on Oct. 1, 1896, simultaneously on five routes from Charlestown, Uvilla, and Halltown, W. Va. Became permanent in 1902.

Special delivery service authorized by act of March 3, 1885. Established October, 1885.

Special-request envelopes first issued in 1865.

Stamped envelopes first issued June 1853 under act of Aug. 31, 1852.

D. Acronyms of Postal Programs

In an effort to streamline the mailstream, the Post Office Department came out with a number of alphabet plans. Some of these follow:

ABCD—Accelerated Business Collection and Delivery. Under this system, mail deposited by 11 A.M. was to be delivered by 3 P.M. within the district of mailing. (Discontinued in 1970.)

FACTS—Facilities Action Control Target System. A computerized information system permitting timely management review of the department's realty program.

MOM—Military Official Mail. To be airlifted on a space available basis.

NIMS—Nationwide Improved Mail Service. Started in 1961, to improve service to commercial mailers.

PAL—Parcel Airlift for overseas military destination packages weighing up to thirty pounds, paid at surface rate plus one dollar surcharge.

POMSIP—A program started in 1962, taking its name from the first letter of each word in Post Office Management and Service Improvement Program.

PROMPT—Program to Record Official Mail to Point Times. A record of time required for movement of mail from patron to delivery point.

PULSE—Property Utilization and Logistics, Supplies and Equipment. A centralized system of material procurement, distribution, utilization and financial control; centralized property accounting; and maintenance management.

SAM—Space Available Mail. Prepaid at surface rates, to, from or between overseas military personnel; to be airlifted on a space available basis.

SCF—Sectional Center Facility. Via this system, inaugurated in 1961, routing is keyed to 552 Sectional Centers serving from forty to seventy post offices each, with practically all of the transportation from Sectional Centers by truck.

SPEED—Scheduled Procurement of Essential Equipment Deliveries. A program started in 1968 to speed the buying of mail mechanization equipment.

TEAM—Team Effectiveness Approach to Management. A training program for management personnel begun in 1970.

VIM—Vertical Improved Mail. A program started in 1963, to speed mail into, through, and out of business buildings.

ZIP—Zone Improvement Plan. A numerical code, inaugurated in 1963, showing geographical area, mail facility and route from which the address is delivered.

E.   Reorganization Facts and Figures
(As of July 1, 1971)

Post Offices

The Postal Service had 32,002 post offices.* There were 4,997 first class post offices; 7,331 second class; 12,641 third class; and 7,053 fourth class. In addition there were 11,110 contract and classified stations, branches and rural stations.

The twenty-five largest post offices, listed from highest receipts (over $300 million) to lowest receipts (less than $30 million) were (1) New York, (2) Chicago, (3) Los Angeles, (4) Philadelphia, (5) Boston, (6) San Francisco, (7) Washington, (8) Detroit, (9) Dallas, (10) St. Louis, (11) Cleveland, (12) Kansas City, (13) Brooklyn, (14) Atlanta, (15) Minneapolis, (16) Houston, (17) Pittsburgh, (18) Baltimore, (19) Cincinnati, (20) Milwaukee, (21) Indianapolis, (22) Dayton, (23) Denver, (24) Miami, (25) Seattle.

Volume

During F.Y. 1971, the department delivered 84.9 billion pieces of mail. This was broken down by classes:
First class (personal and business)—48.6 billion pieces.

* At the end of fiscal 1968, there were 32,261 post offices, the lowest total since 1872. The number decreased each succeeding year: F.Y. 1969, 32,064; and F.Y. 1970, 32,039.

Domestic airmail—1.5 billion pieces.
Second class (newspapers and magazines)—9.4
    billion pieces.
Third class (commercial)—20 billion pieces.
Fourth class—977 million pieces.
Penalty—2.5 billion pieces.
Other (Free for the blind, franked, controlled
    circulation publications)—2 billion pieces.
As the largest postal organization in the world, the
United States Post Office had an annual volume equal to
almost half of the world's total. In other words, on a
typical day, the United States Post Office processed al-
most as much mail as the rest of the world combined.

Space

In its major facilities, the Postal Service occupied a
total of 147,000,000 square feet of space, and it used
62,500,000 square feet in 3,095 other Federal buildings.
Another 70,000,000 sq. ft. were under lease in about
11,000 buildings. Finally, 13,000,000 sq. ft. were rented
in another 16,000 buildings throughout the country.

Deliveries

City carriers served 51,549,916 families and 4,798,-
538 businesses along 130,387 city routes. Rural carriers
served 11,089,556 families along 31,346 rural routes.

Money Orders

The Postal Service issued and paid about 200 million
money orders in the United States and 500,000 for payment abroad. Revenues from money orders was about
$60 million.

Number of Employees

Headquarters   3,000

Field Regular Employees

Regional Administrative Offices	8,000	
Inspection Service	3,000	
Postmasters	31,000	
Supervisors and Technicians	38,000	
Clerks and Mail Handlers	244,000	
City Carriers and Vehicle Drivers	163,000	
Rural Carriers	31,000	
Special Delivery Messengers	3,000	
Bldg. and Equipment Maintenance	21,000	
Vehicle Maintenance	5,000	
Regular Employees		547,000
Substitute Employees		200,000
Grand Total		750,000

F.   Synopsis of the Postal Reorganization Act of 1970

H.R. 17070, upon being signed by President Nixon on August 12, 1970, became known as the Postal Reorganization Act. It contains 15 sections. Following is a condensed version of each section.

Section I: The Act is to be cited as the Postal Reorganization Act.

Section II: Revises and reenacts the provisions of Title 39, USC. Discussed separately in Section XV.

Section III: Provides for the continuation of existing postal rates and fees.

Section IV: Provides for the transfer to the United States Postal Service of all the functions, powers, and duties of the Post Office Department and the Postmaster General, and abolishes the Post Office Department and the office of the Postmaster General of the Post Office Department.

Section V: Contains the "savings" clause providing for the continuation of all rules, regulations, permits, contracts, certificates, licenses, privileges, etc., issued by the Post Office Department under the U.S. Postal Service.

Section VI: Contains technical amendments to portions of the existing code. Defines Postal Service as meaning the United States Postal Service established under Title 39.

Section VII: Provides for the study of the private

214

express statutes and that a report on the modernization of the private express statutes will be made to the President and Congress within two years after effective date of this section.

Section VIII: Transfers all officers and employees of the Post Office Department to the United States Postal Service, except for the Postmaster General, Deputy Postmaster General, Assistant Postmasters General, and General Counsel.

Section IX: Provides for increase in pay rates of 8% retroactive to first pay period beginning on or after April 16, 1970.

Section X: Provides for the negotiation of wages, hours, and working conditions of employees between national unions and management. States that such negotiation must include compressibility of pay steps to eight years maximum. States that negotiations will commence not later than thirty days after requested by either party; if parties fail to reach agreement after ninety days of bargaining, a factfinding panel will be established; and if no agreement after one hundred and eighty days, an arbitration board will be established.

Section XI: Provides for keeping in force of laws that existed prior to the new Postal Service.

Section XII· States that expenses incurred by the Postal Service prior to date of commencement of activities will be borne by the Post Office Department.

Section XIII: Authorizes the Postmaster General to appoint Postmasters to offices of all classes by one of the following three methods applied in order of precedence: (1) selection of qualified employee serving at the post office where the vacancy occurs, including an acting postmaster who was serving on January 1, 1969, who shall acquire a competitive status upon being appointed postmaster, (2) if no qualified employee is available or willing at the post office, by selection of a qualified employee serving in the postal field service, (3) if no qualified employee is available or willing, selection will be by competitive examination in accordance with Title 5, USC governing appointments in the competitive service. States that this enactment will not affect the status or tenure of postmasters in office on the date of enactment of this Act.

Section XIV: States that the mailing of unsolicited sexually oriented advertisements is an invasion of privacy and contrary to public policy.

Section XV: Provides for effective dates of various sections of the Act. Revision of Title 39 U.S. Code (As mentioned in Section II). Title 39 consists of five parts: General, Personnel, Modernization and Fiscal Administration, Mail Matter, and Transportation of Mail. Some highlights are listed below:

201: The U.S. Postal Service is established as an independent establishment of the executive branch of the government of the United States.

202: Provides for a Board of Governors composed of eleven members. Nine of the members, to be known as governors, are to be appointed by the President with not more than five being adherents of the same political party. The governors shall be chosen to represent the public interest generally and shall not be representatives of specific interests using the Postal Service. Salary will be $10,000 per year plus $300 a day for not more than 30 days of meetings each year plus travel and expense reimbursements for attending meetings of the board. Terms will be for nine years, except that terms of governors first taking office shall expire as designated by the President at the time of appointment, one at the end of one year, one at the end of two years, one at the end of three years, etc. The nine governors shall appoint (and may remove) the Postmaster General, who shall be a voting member of the Board. His pay and term of service shall be fixed by the governors. The nine governors and the Postmaster General shall appoint (and may remove) the Deputy Postmaster General, who shall be a voting member of the Board, with pay and term of service fixed by the governors.

203: States that the chief executive officer of the Postal Service is the Postmaster General. The alternate chief executive officer is the Deputy Postmaster General.

204: There will be such numbers of Assistant Postmasters General as the Board shall consider appropriate and a General Counsel and a Judicial Officer. They shall serve at the pleasure of the Postmaster General.

205: The Board of Governors shall direct and control the expenditures and review the practices and policies of the Postal Service, and perform other functions and duties prescribed by the Act. No officer or employee of the United States may serve concurrently as a governor.

206: There shall be a Postal Service Advisory Council, of which the Postmaster General shall be the chairman and the Deputy Postmaster the vice chairman. The Advisory Council shall have eleven additional members appointed by the President. They will be four persons representing labor organizations, four persons representing major mail users, and three persons representing the general public.

207: The seal of the Postal Service shall be filed by the Board in the office of the Secretary of the State, judicially noticed, affixed to all commissions of officers of the Postal Service, and used to authenticate records of the Postal Service.

208: Congress reserves the power to alter, amend, or repeal any or all of the sections of this title.

412: Except as specifically provided by law, no officer or employee of the Postal Service shall make available to the public by any means or for any purpose any mailing or other list of names or addresses (past or present) of postal patrons or other persons.

1001: Employees shall be in the postal career service, a part of the civil service. Appointments and promotions shall be in accordance with procedures established by the Postal Service. Also, the Postal Service may hire executives under employment contracts for periods not in excess of five years.

1002: States that political recommendations will not be considered or accepted in making any type of personnel action.

1203: States that Postal Service shall accord exclusive recognition to a labor organization when the organization has been selected by a majority of the employees in an appropriate unit as their representative.

2003: Establishes in the Treasury a revolving fund to be called the Postal Service Fund which shall be available to the Postal Service without fiscal year limitation to carry out its functions. Receipts and revenues received by the Postal Service will be deposited into this fund.

2005: Authorizes the Postal Service to borrow money and to issue and sell obligations as it determines necessary not to exceed ten billion dollars.

2401: All revenues received by the Postal Service are appropriated to the Postal Service. Appropriations to the Postal Service as reimbursement for public service costs are authorized in an amount equal of ten percent of the FY '71 appropriation, for each year through 1979, with an annual reduction of this reimbursement for each year thereafter.

2402: The Postmaster General must make an annual report to the Board of Governors and the Board will transmit such report to the President and Congress.

3601: Establishes a Postal Rate Commission, composed of five commissioners appointed by the President, not more than three of whom are adherents of the same political party. One of the commissioners shall be designated as chairman. Commissioners will be chosen on the basis of their professional qualifications. They will serve for a six year term. The terms of the initial appointees will be staggered: two years, four years, six years.

3603: Provides that the Postal Rate Commission shall promulgate rules and regulations and establish procedures which will not be subject to any change or supervision by the Postal Service.

3621: The Board of Governors is authorized to establish classes of mail and equitable rates of postage and fees. These shall provide sufficient revenues so that total estimated income and appropriations will equal as nearly as practicable total estimated costs.

3622: The Postal Service shall request a Rate Commission to submit a recommended decision on changes in a rate or fee for postal services if the Service determines that such changes would be in the interest of the public. (Section 3625 states that the governors, upon receiving a recommendation from the Rate Commission, may approve, allow under protest, reject, or modify that decision.)

5007: Provides for free transportation of postal employees on duty in charge of the mails or traveling to and from such duty.

5207: Provides that the ICC shall determine and fix rates for transportation.

Bibliography

This book drew upon many sources—newspaper articles, publications of the Government Printing Office, Civil Service Commission pamphlets, excerpts from the *U.S. Code, Congressional Directories, Congressional Record*, the *Federal Register* and the *International Nomenclature* volumes printed by the Universal Postal Union at Berne, Switzerland. Various publications of the U.S. Post Office Department and U.S. Postal Service, including *Postal Life, Postal Leader*, the *Postal Manual, Postal Bulletins, General Orders, Annual Reports* of the Postmasters General, *Directory of Post Offices* and all of the employee organizations' publications such as the *Postal Supervisor*, the *Postal Transport Journal*, The *Postmaster's Advocate*, the *National Rural Letter Carrier*, and the *Postal Record*, were consulted. The following books were helpful and would be of interest to those fascinated by postology.

Bailey, Thos. A. *The American Pageant*, Boston: Little, Brown & Co., 1956.

Buggs, Winthrop S. *Foundations of Philately*, Princeton, N.J.: D. Van Nostrand Co., 1955.

Carman, Harry J. *Social and Economic History of the United States*, New York: D. C. Heath & Co., 1930.

Coulter, E. Merton *Confederate States of America*, Baton Rouge: Louisiana State University Press, 1950.

Crane, Verner W. *Benjamin Franklin's Letters to the Press*, Chapel Hill: University of North Carolina Press, 1950.

Cullinan, Gerald *The Post Office Department*, New York: Frederick A. Praeger, 1968.

Day, J. Edward *My Appointed Round*, New York: Holt, Rinehart and Winston, 1965.

Dickerson, O. M. *American Colonial Government*, New York: Russell & Russell, 1962.

Doherty, William *Mailman, U.S.A.*, New York: David McKay Co., 1960.

Donaldson, J. M. *A Wartime History of the Post Office Department*, Washington, D.C.: Government Printing Office, 1961.

Farley, James A. *Jim Farley's Story*, New York: McGraw-Hill, 1968.

Forster, R. K. *Postmark Collecting*, London: Stanley Paul, 1960.

Fuller, Wayne E. *R.F.D.*, Bloomington: Indiana University Press, 1964.

Glines, Carroll V. *The Saga of the Airmail*, Princeton, N.J.: D. Van Nostrand Co., 1968.

Hafen, LeRoy Reuben *Western America*, Englewood Cliffs, N.J.: Prentice-Hall, 1970.

Hahn, Mannel *So You're Collecting Stamps*, New York: Dodd, Mead & Co., 1940.

Harlow, Alvin F. *Paper Chase*, New York: Henry Holt & Co., 1940.

Harrison, Michael and Armstrong, Douglas *A New Approach to Stamp Collecting*, Garden City, N.Y.: Hanover House, 1954.

Herst, Herman, Jr. *Fun and Profit In Stamp Collecting*, New York: Duell, Sloan, and Pierce, 1962.

Herst, Herman, Jr. *Nassau Street*, New York: Duell, Sloan & Pierce, 1963.

Kehr, Ernest A. *The Romance of Stamp Collecting*, New York: Thos. Y. Crowell Co., 1948.

McMaster, John B. *A History of the People of the United States During Lincoln's Administration*, New York: D. Appleton & Co., 1927.

Nicklin, John W. *Fabulous Stamps*, New York: Hastings House, 1939.

Patrick, Douglas *The Postage Stamps and Postal History of the United States*, Toronto: Ryerson Press, 1955.

President's Commission on Postal Organization *Towards Postal Excellence: The Kappel Commission Report.* Washington, D.C.: Government Printing Office, 1968.

Randel, William Pierce *Centennial: American Life in 1876.* Philadelphia: Chilton Book Co., 1969.

Scheele, Carl H. *A Short History of the Mail Service*, Washington, D.C.: Smithsonian Institution Press, 1970.

Schenk, Gustav *The Romance of the Postage Stamp*, Garden City, N.Y.: Doubleday & Co., 1962.

Schlesinger, Arthur M., Jr. *The Age of Jackson*, Boston: Little, Brown & Co., 1945.

Summerfield, Arthur E. *U.S. Mail*, New York: Holt, Rinehart & Winston, 1960.

Reference Works

Carruth, Gorton and Assoc. *Encyclopedia of American Facts and Dates*, New York: Thos. Y. Crowell Co., 1962.

Dietz Confederate States Catalog and Handbook, Richmond, Va.: Dietz Press, 1959.

Hornung, Otto *The Illustrated Encyclopedia of Stamp Collecting* Middlesex, England: Hamlyn House Feltham, 1970.

Minkus New World Wide Stamp Catalog, New York: Scott Publications, 1960.

U.S. Post Office Department *Postage Stamps of the United States*, Washington, D.C.: Government Printing Office, 1957.

Scott's U.S. Stamp Catalog, Specialized New York: Scott Publications, 1966.

Scott's Standard Postage Stamp Catalog, New York: Scott Publications, 1970.

U.S. Post Office Department *Universal Postal Constitution* and *Convention.* Washington, D.C.: Government Printing Office, 1964.